SCOOKING WITH SEITAN

THE COMPLETE VEGETARIAN "WHEAT-MEAT" COOKBOOK

BARBARA JACOBS
LEONARD JACOBS

Avery Publishing Group

Garden City Park, New York

Cover Photograph: Robert Kaufman, Newton Upper Falls, Massachusetts
Original Seitan Illustrations: Barbara Jacobs
Decorative Artwork: Vicki Rae Chelf and Shea MacKenzie
In-House Editor: Marie Caratozzolo
Typesetter: Bonnie Freid
Printer: Paragon Press, Honesdale, Pennsylvania

The quotation by Alice Waters, found on page xi, has been reprinted with permission.

Publisher's Cataloging in Publication

Jacobs, Barbara.
   Cooking with seitan : the complete vegetarian "wheat-meat" cookbook / Barbara and Leonard Jacobs.
   p. cm.
   Includes bibliographical references and index.
   ISBN 0-89529-599-7

   1. Cookery (Gluten) I. Jacobs, Leonard. II. Title.

TX809.G55J33 1994   641.6'311
                                  QBI94-342

Printed in the United States of America

10 9 8 7 6 5 4 3 2 1

CONTENTS

*This book is dedicated to our parents and children,
from whom we learned the life-affirming qualities
of homemade whole foods.*

ACKNOWLEDGMENTS

In writing a book that is a distillation of wisdom and practical advice from years of experience and study, it is practically impossible to identify all the people who have been the primary sources of information and inspiration. We have learned simple, delicious, and healthful cooking from scores of imaginative and talented people, most of whom were only demonstrating their intuition and common sense. But from these people we have learned practical techniques to share through this book.

The early introduction of healthful natural and whole foods in our lives came from the macrobiotic community in Boston, Massachusetts. The hundreds of people who passed through this community in the late 1960s and early 1970s were dedicated to uncovering the intricate connections between traditional and wholesome foods and our mental and physical health. Searching out these connections led to the rediscovery of traditional food preparation and traditional foods. Seitan was one of these foods.

The Seventh Inn Restaurant, founded by Michio and Aveline Kushi, which opened in Boston in 1971, was a primary source of research and experimentation on traditional health foods. It was at this restaurant that the preparation of seitan was first presented by a young Japanese woman Yumie Kono. She, along with the other creative cooks at the restaurant, deserves acknowledgment by all those who have enjoyed seitan and other healthful foods.

Frank and Marjorie Ford, and the Arrowhead Mills Farm, were among the early pioneers in growing organic whole wheat in America. The excellent supply of whole wheat from the farm was the foundation for preparing seitan as a new and truly healthful food.

Over the past twenty-five years, many people have developed healthful food products using wholesome and natural ingredients. Some of these products are used as ingredients in this cookbook. In addition, there are now many companies making seitan for their local community or for national distribution. We are grateful to these peoples' efforts and want to acknowledge their work as real health food pioneers.

In addition to the food manufacturers, we want to acknowledge those folks who have distributed the information about healthy lifestyles through the printed medium of book publishing. Those adventurous and ambitious book companies who have made it their business to provide books on the value of whole foods have finally found Americans to be a receptive audience, but this has required incredible dedication and perseverance. In particular, our publisher, Avery Publishing Group, and its managing editor, Rudy Shur, deserve especial mention as pioneers and leaders in producing health literature and natural foods cookbooks in America.

Finally we want to acknowledge Jesse, Daria, Joshua, Molly, and Sean Jacobs—our children. Their willing appetites and eagerness to test new recipes and to await their parents' completion of this manuscript deserve particular mention and appreciation. Without them, this book would have no reason for being.

And for all those others who have contributed to the improving quality of food in America, we also recognize and appreciate your efforts. We are witnessing a revolution in food quality in America, and we are thrilled to be sharing this revolution with you.

FOREWORD

In 1983, immediately after delivering *American Wholefoods Cuisine* to our publisher, we embarked on three months R&R, traveling through Asia. Having already been professionally involved with natural foods for fifteen years, our encounters with new foods and techniques were becoming increasingly rare. When we reached Hong Kong, however, a major gap in our education emerged—we were introduced to seitan, a wheat-derived product used extensively in the Orient to create mock meat dishes.

In Hong Kong there are numerous vegetarian restaurants based on the ancient traditions of the Chinese Buddhist monks. The menus in these establishments feature "beef," "pork," "chicken," and "duck," all made from wheat gluten. To our surprise, we often found these items indistinguishable from meat. What impressed us most was the versatility of this food. We believed that seitan could be a great hook for attracting the meat-oriented Western palate to vegetarian cuisine.

Our next serious interlude with seitan was in 1988 at the Unicorn Restaurant in Miami, where we dined on their unforgettable California Seitan. Unlike our first experience, in which the seitan was clearly a substitute for meat, in this dish, the seitan, which was sautéed with garlic and tomatoes and paired with slices of avocado in a delicate brown sauce, succeeded on its own. We were once again reminded that this was a food worth pursuing.

At that time seitan was only sporadically available in natural foods stores. Eager to get a thorough immersion, we decided to make the gluten ourselves. Finding a recipe proved more difficult than the actual preparation. While the basic procedure—preparing a dough, kneading and rinsing it under water until it became an elastic mass, then simmering it in broth—was readily discovered, precise information about timing, yield, shaping, and similar vital details that a novice would find essential was elusive. Nonetheless, we stumbled our way through and it proved to be both simple and fun. Our homemade seitan's major debut was a Thanksgiving dinner. It was far less work than preparing a bird and a big hit with everyone who tried it.

Our on-again off-again relationship with seitan continued as subsequent attempts to prepare gluten from scratch ended in total failure. Unable to discern the error, our foray into seitan met with early demise. In fact, we virtually forgot about this remarkable food until recently, when it appeared on the menu of two local restaurants. One taste and we remembered immediately why we had been so smitten years back.

Naturally, we were delighted to hear that Barbara and Leonard Jacobs had put together a thorough compendium on seitan. Within the first few pages, all the frustrating details we couldn't unearth during our early seitan-making days were illuminated. Finally, here was the information to help guide anyone through each step of the seitan-making process—how to properly mix the dough; how long to knead it, let it rest, and rinse it; and how to transform the flavorless gluten into tasty seitan. After reading the Jacobs' skillful explanations, it was apparent why some of our earlier trials had ended unsuccessfully.

Cooks short of time will be happy to learn that seitan can be purchased ready-made or as a boxed mix. To fill this need, the Jacobs have provided a list of suppliers. On the other hand, those who make their own seitan will reap additional rewards, for in the true spirit of Oriental cooking, where nothing is wasted, even the starch water from making gluten has its uses. For example, the reserved starch water is an essential component of several of the Jacobs' enticing sweet cookies and pudding desserts. But either way, readers are sure to be amazed by the spectrum of dishes that can be created with this versatile food.

Although, happily, the Jacobs don't make a fuss over the following fact, most techniques for preparing seitan—pan-simmering, oven-braising, pressure-cooking, and baking—yield a foodstuff that is extremely low in fat. (The exception is deep-frying, a cooking method that results in a food that is still leaner than most cuts of meat.) As a result, people who are interested in reducing the fat content of their diets without sacrificing taste will find seitan to be one of their best allies. Seitan is also surprisingly convenient since, once prepared, it can be refrigerated or frozen for subsequent use.

We urge those who haven't yet experienced this culinary delight to do so at once, for they have a lot of catching up to do. If you are already familiar with seitan, the Jacobs offer a repertoire of recipes that suffice for a lifetime of enjoyment.

Nikki and David Goldbeck
Authors of *American Wholefoods Cuisine*

PREFACE

This cookbook represents part of a revolution, one that began when inventive cooks started reintroducing whole grains as staple foods in their cooking repertoires. It is the same revolution in which chefs began to discover the remarkable transformative qualities of certain foods such as soybeans and whole wheat. Soybeans, for example, can be converted into tofu, miso, soy sauce, soymilk, and tempeh, while whole wheat can be made into whole grain breads, noodles, pancakes, muffins, and seitan.

In the late 1800s, John Harvey Kellogg and Charles W. Post became pioneers in this movement to redirect the American cuisine. They realized that whole grains such as wheat, corn, rye, and oats—long the staples of many civilizations—added considerable nutritional improvement to the then-popular American diet. Like many others, Post and Kellogg promoted the use of the kitchen as a food laboratory. This encouraged the creation of new foods that bore faint resemblance to their original ingredients. Seitan is such a food.

Seitan begins with whole wheat berries that are ground into flour. This flour is mixed with water and kneaded into an elastic dough. The dough is rinsed under water to dissolve and wash away the starch, leaving the stretchy gluten behind. When cooked, the gluten is transformed into seitan, a food with a texture and flavor quite different from its original ingredients. This is the magic of the cooking process. And this is part of the whole foods revolution.

We feel intimately involved in this movement. For over twenty-five years we have studied, experimented with, and cooked many types of traditional whole foods. We have raised five children primarily on the results of these efforts. Our children, parents, brothers, sisters, and friends have shared our meals over the years. Their response has helped us perfect a whole foods cuisine.

With a culinary emphasis on vegetarian-based meals, our studies in cooking have ranged from European-style peasant dishes to highly refined temple foods of China and Japan. We have managed restaurants, studied cooking with master chefs, and taught cooking to hundreds of students. For nearly two decades, we published the *East West Journal* (now called *Natural Health*), promoted books on the new and natural dietetics, and wrote one of the first books about seitan in 1986.

This brings us to the book you now have in your hands. Although filled with a wide range of delicious kitchen-tested recipes, *Cooking with Seitan* is more than a simple cookbook. It is also a historic, educational, and revolutionary text that centers around a food that is both novel and traditional. Included within this book are illustrated step-by-step instructions for making seitan from scratch. By following these simple instructions, you can transmute dry meal into a succulent, savory food.

If, however, you are reluctant to create your own homemade seitan, be aware that instant seitan mixes, as well as commercially prepared seitan are available in many natural foods stores. These convenient products allow you to take advantage of the multitude of recipes offered in this book.

The first few chapters of *Cooking with Seitan* present a wide variety of information. Included is a look at wheat's role through the ages, and the rising popularity of seitan. Step-by-step instructions are presented for making seitan from scratch, beginning with the extraction of gluten from various types of whole wheat flour. Also offered are the basic herb-and-spice combinations used to flavor seitan varieties. These seasoning blends create meat-like flavors for this totally vegetarian food. Finally, basic cooking methods for creating a variety of textures are described.

The main section of the book includes a myriad of easy-to-follow seitan recipes that require basic procedures and simple cooking methods. From soups, snacks, and appetizers to casseroles, salads, and desserts, unusual and delicious recipes are offered to satisfy even the most discriminating palates. As an added bonus, most of the recipes can be prepared in a short period of time. A few dishes may require extra preparation or special attention but are worth the added effort. You may choose to prepare the more intricate, involved recipes for special occasions—an age-old tradition in itself.

We can assure you that all of the recipes have been tested in our own kitchen, and have been tasted and endorsed by family and friends. We wish you similar success, and hope that through cooking with seitan, you experience a sense of accomplishment and discovery. There is a unique pleasure in carrying on this ancient tradition, and in creating this delicious and healthy food.

Alice Waters, chef and owner of the restaurant Chez Panisse in Berkeley, California, is a major contributor to the movement toward healthy modern American cooking. We agree with her revolutionary credo:

> I still believe from the bottom of my heart that good food is a right, not a privilege. What you eat can change your life. It nourishes our spirits as well as our bodies. Good food—pure and wholesome food, honestly grown, and simply cooked— may be the best hope to transform our society and our consciousness. It matters profoundly.

We sincerely hope that this book, and this simple food, can play some part in the return to a more healthy society. Unrefined, simple peasant fare, which provides a wide range of complex, nutritional, and nourishing elements (unavailable in a modern refined-foods diet), can have a profound effect on our lives. The preparation and consumption of simple meals made from whole foods can be an important first step in bringing us back to a place of balance and harmony. *Cooking with Seitan* is our contribution to this growing movement toward nutritional whole foods cooking.

INTRODUCTION

Whole foods cooks often try to improve upon current culinary techniques. They commonly search out healthful ingredients and cooking methods common to other cultures. From the culinary traditions of Asia, Africa, and South America, valuable and nutritious foods have been discovered, foods that provide excellent counterpoints to the modern Western diet. As a nation, we are reducing our consumption of saturated fats and animal foods, and are returning to a diet that includes a greater quantity of grains and vegetables—a diet that had been common in America before World War II. This dietary reformation is making a major difference in the overall health-consciousness of the American people.

Seitan is part of this process toward dietary reform. A food rich in complex carbohydrates and low in fat, seitan has a long and interesting tradition rooted in various cultures throughout the world. This unique food can play an important part in improving the modern American cuisine.

In the late 1970s, tofu—the remarkable and versatile soy food—was little known outside of a few select natural foods stores and Asian markets. However, within the twelve years following its introduction, this healthful natural food established itself as a major component of the modern American diet. Due to the work of a few dedicated and health-conscious food pioneers, tofu is now found in most supermarkets throughout the United States. From Boston to

Los Angeles, and from Seattle to Miami, tofu has been adopted as an all-American health food. As the search for alternatives to fatty and refined cholesterol-rich foods continues, tofu remains an essential part of a healthy diet.

In a similar fashion, seitan—the extracted and flavored gluten from whole wheat—stands a good chance of becoming the next newly discovered traditional American health food. Tasty and unique, seitan is just now gaining popularity in the American diet.

Although long a staple in Asia (and some European countries), seitan has only recently become available outside of a few natural foods stores. In 1970, when we first tasted seitan, it was a tasty but exotic snack food, owing its extremely salty flavor to the fact that it was an imported Japanese specialty food, flavored for the Japanese taste. In addition to being heavily salted, this seitan was hard, chewy, and quite expensive. It was really just a snack food to be eaten while drinking beer. Unfortunately, no one involved in the natural foods movement in this country was familiar with the methods used to make this food.

In 1971, Leonard became the head chef at the Seventh Inn, one of Boston's first natural foods restaurants. During that time, he and I began our search for different traditional food-preparation techniques and studied with experts in all areas of cooking and baking. In March 1971, a young Japanese woman named Yumie Kono came to work at the Seventh Inn. It was Yumie who taught us how to make seitan. Even macrobiotics leaders Michio and Aveline Kushi—experts in the preparation of healthy Japanese foods—had never actually made seitan from scratch.

Soon, many of the cooks at the Seventh Inn had mastered the technique of making seitan from scratch and began experimenting with ways to create new flavors and textures for this unique food. Of course, the customers at the restaurant were thrilled to test the "experiments," and soon seitan had made a formal entry into the natural foods cuisine. Seitan, in all its forms—hearty entrée, salty snack, savory sandwich filling, and novel dessert ingredient—became one of the most popular foods at the Seventh Inn. And as the cooks and students of the cooks left Boston in the early 1970s, they took with them the recipe for making this unique food. Soon seitan shops were opening up throughout the United States and Europe.

Jonathan's Seitan Shop in Antwerp, Belgium has an interesting background. Jonathan Van de Ponseele, the son of a Belgian butcher, took over his father's butcher shop and ran it in the style of his father. In 1975, Jonathan discovered the value of a macrobiotic and natural foods diet and transformed his butcherie into a seitan shop, creating seitan with the flavors and textures of many varieties of his meats. This shop continues today both as a retail store and as a manufacturer and distributor of "Jonathan's Seitan," which is sold throughout Western Europe.

In the mid-1970s, a seitan product called "tan pups" had become a most popular snack food. Created in Boston, tan pups were similar to the county fair specialty of dough-covered hot dogs on a stick. Tan pups were pieces of seitan that had been dipped in flavored batter and deep-fried. Boston area natural foods stores carried these healthy snacks as staple items.

When we searched out the origin of seitan, we discovered that it had been a staple food among vegetarian monks of China, Russian wheat farmers, peasants of Southeast Asia, and Mormons. People who had traditionally eaten wheat had also discovered a method to extract the gluten and create a seitan-like product.

Like baking bread at home, making seitan provides the enjoyment of transforming whole wheat flour into a food with a unique flavor and texture that is far different from its original consistency. The satisfaction of making a food from scratch that you know is tasty, satisfying, and extremely healthful is a definite incentive.

Many natural foods stores sell frozen seitan entrées, as well as fresh seitan that comes in sealed tubs (like tofu). Instant seitan mixes, which require you to simply add water, mix, and cook, are also available.

Seitan is a truly remarkable food that is on its way to becoming the "tofu of the 90s." With a little effort and an adventurous spirit, you might discover seitan to be a well-liked and flavorful addition to your diet. Take this book along with some whole wheat flour, and start on an adventure to expand your cuisine while satisfying your appetite for delicious and healthful food.

1

A NEWLY DISCOVERED ANCIENT FOOD

Plain cooking cannot be trusted to plain cooks.

—Countess Morphy

What is it about seitan that makes it so unique? Its versatility? Its ability to adapt to an amazing range of flavors and textures? For us, the phenomenon of transforming a simple flour-and-water mixture into a remarkably versatile and delicious food is what makes seitan so fascinating. Like tofu, seitan begins with a relatively neutral taste but, depending on how it is cooked and seasoned, is capable of taking on a wide range of textures and flavors. The versatility of seitan allows cooks to recreate some of their favorite meat dishes in a revised vegetarian mode. Seitan can even be used to make delicious desserts!

A TRADITIONAL FOOD

Seitan is a food with a long history. Although not widely known in the West, seitan has been traditional fare in China, Korea, Japan, Middle Eastern countries, and most other places where wheat is a staple product. In North America, the Mormons and the Seventh-day Adventists eat seitan frequently.

Seitan—gluten that has been extracted from wheat flour and then cooked—comes to the United States from Japan, where it was prepared originally by vegetarian Buddhist monks. It is also known simply as gluten or "wheat meat"; however, we prefer to use the Japanese name even though technically the word seitan refers to gluten that has been cooked in soy sauce.

According to Yuko Okada, president of Muso Company, Ltd., one of the oldest and largest exporters of Japanese natural foods, the word "seitan" was coined in the mid-1960s by macrobiotics teacher George Ohsawa. The word "sei" means *is* and "tan," which is the first character in the word tanpaku, means *protein*. So seitan, loosely translated, means something like *the right protein substitute*.

The Chinese call wheat gluten "mien chin" or "yu mien ching." Chinese restaurants often refer to wheat gluten as "Buddha food," due to the claim that it was originally developed by Buddhist monks. Oriental foods markets also offer a dried wheat gluten called "fu" by the Japanese and "k'o fu" or "kofu" by the Chinese.

The commercial production of seitan began in 1962 by Kiyoshi Mokutani of the Marushima Shoyu Company. Mokutani developed the product for George Ohsawa and his macrobiotics students. It was the vegetarian form of a condiment popularly made from shellfish. By the late 1960s, Marushima-manufactured seitan was being exported to the United States. This original Japanese seitan was quite salty. It was an excellent snack food, as well as a seasoning for bean and vegetable dishes.

William Shurtleff, author of *The Book of Tofu* and *The Book of Miso*, is largely responsible for introducing tofu to the American natural foods cuisine. In his new book, *Sourcebook on Wheat Gluten Foods and Seitan* (Soyfoods Center, 1992), Shurtleff presents a historical overview of the development and value of wheat gluten and seitan as staple foods.

Shurtleff feels that products made from wheat gluten will be particularly appealing in the American and European diets as people continue to reduce their consumption of animal foods, yet crave high-protein foods with a meaty texture and flavor. (Seitan more closely resembles beef than any soy-based food.) As an added bonus, seitan contains absolutely no fat.

WHEAT—THE SOURCE

The nutritional, healthful qualities of seitan can be traced to its primary ingredient—wheat.

Wheat has been around since prehistoric times. The oldest grains, dating from 6750 B.C., were discovered in excavations in the area of

Iraq known as the "fertile crescent." Since ancient times, wheat has been an important cereal grain in almost every country of the Western world. The history of cultivated wheat and human civilization are closely interwoven.

Wheat contains a large proportion of essential nutrients: 60 to 80 percent carbohydrates, 8 to 15 percent protein, 1.5 to 2 percent minerals, and vitamins such as B-complex and E. In addition to its high nutritive value, wheat has a low water content, making it easy to transport, process, and store. These qualities have made wheat the most important staple food of more than 1 billion people (or 35 percent of the world's population).

Wheat is classified into different types according to planting schedules and endosperm compositions. Spring wheat is planted, like most crops, in the springtime. Winter wheat is planted in the fall, and lives through the winter as a small plant that sends up its flowering stalks in the spring. Soft, hard, and durum (hardest) wheats are classified according to the mechanical strength of the kernel, which, in turn, is a result of the protein-to-starch ratio in the endosperm. Hard wheats contain fewer and smaller starch grains, resulting in a stronger, more continuous protein matrix.

The hard wheats, because of their higher gluten content, are the types generally used to make seitan. In classical Roman times, hard wheat was referred to as *triticum* and the soft was called *silgo*. The hard spring wheats usually have a bit more gluten than the hard winter varieties.

When ground and mixed with water, wheat protein forms gluten—a complex, semi-solid elastic structure. Gluten dough can stretch under pressure yet tends to resist that pressure. It expands to accommodate gases that are produced by yeast, yet it contains the gases instead of stretching to the point of bursting.

As wheat varieties have different protein-to-starch ratios, certain varieties are better suited for specific products. Durum is the hardest type of wheat. It is too hard for making bread and seitan, which need some "give." Durum is usually milled into a flour called semolina, which is good for making the very stiff dough necessary for dried pasta. Soft-wheat varieties have a high-starch content and develop weak gluten. Soft wheat is generally made into cake flour and used in products that are meant to be tender and crumbly, such as pastries and biscuits. Often, soft wheat is combined with harder varieties for breadmaking. Pastry wheat, a white spring variety, is very low in gluten content and is best used for crackers and pastry dough. Pastry wheat is commonly used by the Japanese to make udon noodles.

Table 1.1   Analysis of Wheat Varieties

Type	Protein %	Starch %	Sugar %	Fat %	Ash %
Hard Red Spring	16.5	61.2	3.19	2.0	2.04
Durum	16.0	63.0	3.58	2.19	2.19
Hard Red Winter	15.3	63.5	2.84	1.67	1.92
Soft Red Winter	12.4	66.5	2.90	1.66	2.07
Soft Red Spring	11.2	66.6	4.02	1.80	1.86
Soft White Spring	7.5	79.4	2.90	1.71	1.92

Chemical analysis reveals a definite difference in the composition of the various types of wheat. Table 1.1 illustrates these differences.

The hard-wheat varieties contain larger amounts of protein than the soft varieties. Yet, this in itself does not explain the great differences in the baking properties of the two types of flour. These differences are attributed to the nature of the proteins in the endosperm. Evidence shows that there is a higher ratio of soluble protein to insoluble protein in the endosperm of soft wheat; hard wheat contains more insoluble protein (gluten).

The endosperm of wheat consists of thin-walled cells that are embedded in protein. This elastic protein, which can be developed into gluten, is the source of glutamic acid (the source of monosodium glutamate). Gluten is made up of gliadin and glutenin, which form a chainlike molecule that creates an elastic network.

When wheat flour is first mixed with water, the proteins are in big knotted clumps. Kneading the dough breaks up these clumps and works the proteins into a thin, strong, resilient fabric that is referred to as the gluten sheet. The kneaded dough is like a cellulose sponge, with its holes sealed by the elastic and absorbent gluten.

Gluten is the skeleton of the dough and largely determines its physical character. Glutenin gives the gluten solidity; it is a long, negatively charged molecule and has little taste. Gliadin, which is positively charged, is a soft, sticky substance that is responsible for binding the gluten. Gliadin sticks to the glutenin and prevents it from being washed away in the gluten-extraction process. The gluten and gliadin contain all of the wheat's amino acids.

These details about the chemical composition of gluten may be of interest to only technically minded cooks. However, what makes wheat gluten interesting to everyone who experiences it is its remarkable versatility as an ingredient in a wide variety of dishes. In addition, extracting the sticky gluten from wheat flour then transforming it into a delicious food—seitan—is an amazing experience. Get ready to enjoy this truly unique, healthful food with its fantastic range of flavors and textures.

2
MAKING YOUR OWN SEITAN

Seeing is deceiving.
It's eating that's believing.

James Thurber
Further Fables for Our Times

Seitan is an amazing food. It can be shaped into many different forms and can acquire any one of a vast array of flavors and textures. From savory appetizers to hearty entrées, for use in soups, salads, and even desserts, seitan will hold a special place in your culinary repertoire. Instant seitan mixes and commercially prepared seitan, available in most natural foods stores, make it easy and convenient to prepare seitan dishes. If you have an adventurous spirit, you will want to try your hand at making seitan from scratch. Although time-consuming, making seitan is a surprisingly simple process.

There are many advantages to making seitan from scratch. First, and possibly the greatest, is the satisfaction you can achieve through the creative process of food preparation. Another important advantage is an economical one. Commercially prepared seitan is more costly than homemade. In addition, by choosing your own combination of flours and seasonings, you can create seitan with a greater variety of flavors and textures than what is available commercially.

In order to create seitan, you must first make gluten (seitan in its uncooked form). This chapter provides two recipes for making homemade gluten. One recipe illustrates the traditional gluten-making method (see page 13), while the other offers a quicker homemade version (see page 18). Once prepared, the raw gluten is then shaped, seasoned, and cooked in any one of a variety of ways to produce seitan.

9

The flour used can be high-gluten whole wheat bread flour, or any of a number of combinations of whole wheat, unbleached white, and extracted gluten flour. These flours can be used individually or in combinations, but the basic method of preparing seitan follows the same general procedure regardless of the type of flour used. Table 2.1 shows different flour combinations and their resulting seitan textures.

Choosing the correct flour is essential for successful homemade seitan. The whole wheat flour we have found to work best is Arrow-

Table 2.1 Ingredient Combinations for Creating Gluten

Texture Types	Whole Wheat Flour	Unbleached White Flour	Gluten Flour	Water or Other Liquid	Additional Ingredients	Gluten Yield (uncooked seitan)	Best Uses
Medium to very firm	4 cups plus OR 8 cups whole wheat flour	4 cups	—	3½–4 cups	—	2½ cups	All basic preparation forms (cutlets, cubes, strips)
Medium firm	8 cups	—	—	4–5 cups	—	2½ cup	Pouches or stretchable gluten wrappers
Firm and chewy	1⅓ cups plus OR 2⅔ cups either whole wheat "or" unbleached white flour	1⅓ cups	⅔ cup	2–2½ cups	—	2 cups	Ground seitan, plus all basic forms (cutlets, cubes, strips)
Very firm and chewy	—	—	2 cups	1¼ cups water or cooled seasoned stock; 3 tbsp. natural soy sauce; 1 tbsp. sesame or olive oil	Seasoning as desired, added to gluten flour*	2½ cups	Sausage-style links
Soft	—	—	2 cups	1 cup cooled seasoned stock; 1 cup plain soymilk	Seasonings as desired, added to gluten flour*	2 cups	Dumplings and deep-fried puffs

*When using gluten flour only, mix the seasonings directly into the flour instead of adding them to the liquid in which the gluten is to be cooked.

head Mills brand hard red winter wheat flour. However, most brands of whole wheat and unbleached white flour are adequate for most seitan recipes. Vital Wheat Gluten, also from Arrowhead Mills, is our choice for gluten flour.

RECOMMENDED INGREDIENTS

Due to their quality, taste, and healthfulness, certain products are recommended when making seitan and seitan dishes. The following ingredients are used in the recipes throughout this book.

Arrowroot. A starch flour processed from the root of a tropical plant, arrowroot is used primarily as a thickening agent for stews, sauces, and gravies. Arrowroot is preferable to cornstarch as it is a natural food that is processed using a simple method, whereas cornstarch is chemically extracted.

Burdock. A hardy plant that grows wild, burdock root is delicious in soups, stews, and vegetable dishes. It is a good source of vitamin B, and is highly regarded in macrobiotic cooking for its strengthening qualities.

Couscous. Partly refined cracked wheat, couscous, which is available in "white" or whole wheat form, cooks in just a few minutes. Its light texture and delicate flavor make it a favorite part of a nutritious meal.

Ginger. This fragrant, golden-colored root is used fresh as a garnish or seasoning in many Oriental-style dishes.

Kombu. This thick, dark green sea vegetable is a type of kelp. Rich in minerals, kombu is often used to flavor bean and vegetable dishes, as well as soups and stews. In this book, it is primarily called for to flavor seitan cooking broth.

Kuzu. A white starch that is processed from the root of the wild kuzu (also kudzu) plant, this thickening agent is used in sauces, gravies, and some desserts. Like arrowroot, kuzu is a naturally derived product that is preferred over cornstarch.

Mirin. This is a sweet rice wine traditionally made by a complex distillation and double-fermentation process. Mirin is used in cooking as a high-quality sweetener and seasoning.

Miso. This is a protein-rich fermented bean paste made from soybeans, usually with the addition of barley or brown or white rice.

✺ About Flours

We have standardized our recipes using Arrowhead Mills hard red winter wheat flour. You may, however, use various combinations of unbleached white flour and whole wheat flour to create glutens with different textures (see Table 2.1). Most flour varieties found in supermarkets and natural foods stores are suitable.

Miso is commonly used in soup stocks and as a seasoning. When consumed on a regular basis, it aids circulation and digestion.

Nondairy beverages. *See* Rice Dream beverage; Soymilk.

Rice Dream beverage. This versatile nondairy beverage from Imagine Foods is made from brown rice. Rice Dream's rich flavor and light consistency make it a good ingredient in soups, sauces and gravies, and a wide variety of entrées. Original and Vanilla flavors are called for in this book.

Sake. Sake is a fermented rice wine. Usually served warm as a beverage, sake is also used to flavor a variety of Oriental-style dishes.

Sea salt. Unlike rock salt, which is mined from inland beds, sea salt comes from evaporated sea water. Sun-baked or kiln-baked, sea salt is high in trace minerals and contains no dextrose or other chemical additives.

Sea vegetables. Any of a variety of marine plants used as food, sea vegetables are a prime source of vitamins, minerals, and trace elements.

Shoyu. A traditional, naturally fermented soy sauce, shoyu is made from cultured wheat and soybeans, water, and sea salt.

Soymilk. Used extensively in the recipes found in this book, soymilk is an excellent ingredient in soups, sauces, and gravies. It is low in fat and sugars yet rich in protein. There are many varieties of soymilk from which to choose; the recipes in this book have been developed using Edensoy Creamy Original and Vanilla flavors. Edensoy products are produced by American Soy Products.

Tahini. This nut butter is obtained by grinding hulled sesame seeds to a smooth and creamy consistency.

Tamari. A wheat-free, naturally fermented soy sauce, tamari is made from cultured soybeans, water, and sea salt.

Thickening agents. *See* Arrowroot; Kuzu.

Tofu. Tofu is the soybean curd made from soybeans and nigari (an extract from dehydrated sea water). Commonly used in soups, vegetable dishes, and dressings, tofu is high in protein, low in fat, and cholesterol-free.

Umeboshi. Umeboshi are tart, salty Japanese pickled plums usually used in salad dresssings or sauces. They tend to stimulate the appetite and aid digestion. Shiso leaves impart a reddish color and natural flavoring to the plums during pickling. Umeboshi are used either whole or in paste form.

MAKING HOMEMADE SEITAN—
A TWO-STEP PROCESS

The following information details the two steps that are necessary for creating seitan—making the gluten (uncooked seitan) and cooking the gluten.

STEP 1 MAKING THE GLUTEN

The first step in creating seitan is to prepare the gluten, which is called seitan once it is cooked. Detailed, easy-to-follow instructions for creating gluten are presented in the Traditional Homemade Gluten recipe below. A second recipe, Quick Homemade Gluten (page 18), provides an alternate method.

TRADITIONAL
HOMEMADE GLUTEN

YIELD:
2–2½ cups gluten
(1¼–1 ½ pounds)

In this recipe, a combination of whole wheat and unbleached white flour is used to make the gluten. For gluten made from other flour combinations, refer to Table 2.1 on page 10.

4 cups whole wheat flour
4 cups unbleached white flour
3½ cups water

1. In a large bowl, combine the flours and mix to blend them thoroughly.
2. Add the water to the flour 1–2 cups at a time, mixing well with a wooden spoon after each addition (Figure 2.1). When all the water has been added, mix the dough with one hand while holding the bowl steady with the other. (Doing this in the sink will make it easier to add more water as needed to prevent the dough from sticking to your mixing hand.)

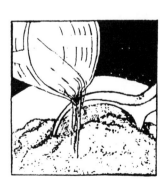

Figure 2.1
*Add water to flours
and mix well.*

3. Knead the dough 50–60 times (Figure 2.2). If the dough is too stiff, add up to ½ cup more water while kneading. Cover the bowl with a damp cloth and let the dough rest 20–30 minutes, allowing the gluten to develop further. (Do not rush this stage. If the gluten does not develop well, much of it will be washed away during the rinsing stage.)

4. With wet hands, knead the dough 10–20 times. The dough, while still fairly soft, should be much more dense and elastic than it had been.

5. Place the bowl of dough in the sink. Add lukewarm water in a gentle stream. As the bowl fills with water, carefully lift one section of the dough at a time and squeeze it slowly but firmly with both hands (Figure 2.3). This manipulation will cause the starch and bran to separate from the gluten. Repeat this squeezing motion about 15 times under the stream of water.

6. Turn off the water and continue to knead the dough. The water will become very thick and cloudy as the starch is released from the dough. Pour off this starch-bran mixture into a container (Figure 2.4) and add fresh cold water to the bowl. Continue this process, alternating between warm- and cold-water rinses, kneading to extract the cream-colored starch. Reserve the starch water from the first few rinses and use it as an ingredient in bread recipes or as a thickener for sauces and stews (see Save That Starch Water! beginning on page 23).

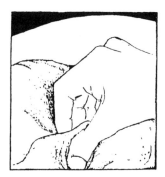

Figure 2.2
Knead the dough.

Figure 2.3
Pick up a section of dough and squeeze it under running water.

Figure 2.4
Pour the starch water into a cup or bowl.

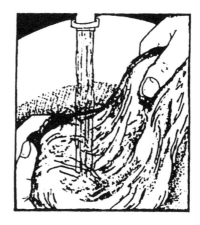

Figure 2.5
*Vigorously pull and stretch
the gluten under running water.*

Figure 2.6
*Knead the mound
of gluten in a colander.*

7. After two complete cycles of kneading the dough and pouring off the starchy water, the dough can be handled more vigorously. Continue kneading and rinsing. You will recognize the emerging gluten by its stringy, elastic quality. Increase the strength of the water stream and the vigor of your squeezing until you are stretching and pulling the gluten in all possible directions (Figure 2.5). Alternate the water temperature; warm water makes the gluten soft, while cold water makes it firm. The gluten will develop into a cohesive mass more quickly as more clear water is worked through the dough, so either knead the dough in a colander under clear, running water (Figure 2.6) or change the water in the bowl often.

8. After about six rinses, the dough will become rubbery gluten. Remaining specks of bran or starch can be rinsed away under the tap by pulling the gluten apart and exposing the inside. Check your progress by squeezing the gluten away from the running water. Any water coming from the gluten should be clear. When it is well washed, the gluten will be shiny and have a firm, elastic consistency. It there is too much bran or starch remaining in the gluten, when cooked, its texture will not be smooth.

9. At this point, the gluten can be cooked, refrigerated, or frozen.

Q&A
About Gluten
and Seitan

Answers to some commonly asked questions regarding homemade gluten and seitan are presented below.

Q: *Why did I get such a low yield of gluten when I tried to make it from scratch? It was wet and stringy, with strands that didn't stick together.*

A: You may have used a low-gluten flour, or flour that was either ground too coarsely or was too fresh. It is also possible that you didn't knead the dough enough, or allow enough time for the dough to rest (see Step 3 of Traditional Homemade Gluten recipe, page 14). Also, you may have kneaded the dough too vigorously during the initial rinsing stage, or rinsed the dough with water that was too warm.

Q: *When making gluten, how will I know if I am kneading the dough too vigorously?*

A: Either the dough will break up in the early rinsing stage, or it will turn into batter and end up down the drain. Remember, during this initial rinsing stage, do not pull the dough apart, rather squeeze it firmly yet gently between your palms.

Q: *When I cooked the gluten, the result was seitan with a sticky, gummy texture. Why?*

A: You didn't wash all the starch from the gluten. During the final rinsing stages, squeeze the gluten away from the running water. The water coming from the gluten should be clear.

Q: *There are so many different types of flour on the market, how can I determine which ones are best for making gluten? I can remember once using a product labeled "bread flour," which disintegrated as I tried to knead it.*

A: In many cases, the "disintegration" problem lies with the flour (even some "bread flours"). There is, however, a simple way to determine which flours work best. Purchase small amounts of several types of whole wheat flour and unbleached white flour. Label the flours to identify their type and place of purchase. Make a small sample batch of gluten with each. Doing this will determine how well each type of flour develops gluten when it is mixed with water, kneaded, allowed to rest, and then rinsed. When you have decided which flour yields the firmest, smoothest, highest-yielding gluten, make a note of it for future purchases. (All of the gluten samples can be cooked together in the same broth.)

Q: *How much gluten should I expect to get from 1 pound of whole wheat flour?*

A: Most commercial seitan manufacturers claim to use flour that produces at least 50 percent gluten by weight, before adding water. So, 1 pound of flour produces approximately ½ pound of gluten, which yields about ¾ pounds of seitan (due to the absorption of cooking water).

Q: *Is there any way I can test the gluten level of wheat flour?*

A: The technical test used by bakers is as follows: First, weigh 1 ounce of flour and add sufficient water to make a ball of dough. Completely immerse the dough ball in a cup of cold water for one hour, allowing the gluten to form. Knead the dough under running water to remove the starch. Weigh the wet gluten on filter paper and record the weight. Place the gluten in a 200°F oven until it is quite dry (this could take more than a couple of hours). Weigh the dry gluten. As a rule, wet gluten weighs about three times more than dry gluten. If this ratio is less, the gluten is of a higher concentration.

QUICK HOMEMADE GLUTEN

YIELD:
2–2½ cups gluten
(1¼–1½ pounds)

A time-saving way to make gluten is by using gluten flour only. Gluten flour, which comes from wheat, contains no starch or bran. When it is the only flour used to make gluten, the kneading and rinsing stages (necessary in the traditional recipe) are eliminated.

2 cups gluten flour
1 cup cool water or seasoned stock
1 cup plain soymilk

1. Place the flour in a large bowl, and add all of the liquid at once. Mix the ingredients immediately and vigorously with a fork to form the dough. When the dough becomes thick and stiff, knead it with your hands 10–15 times.
2. Let the dough rest 2–5 minutes, then knead it a few more times. Allow the gluten to rest about 15 minutes.
3. At this point, the gluten can be cooked, refrigerated, or frozen.

USING A FOOD PROCESSOR TO MAKE GLUTEN DOUGH

You can prepare the dough for gluten in a food processor or heavy-duty mixer, rather than knead it by hand. However, it can take a long time to clean the machine afterward.

When using a food processor or mixer, follow the manufacturer's instructions for making bread dough. If you use the ingredient proportions given in this chapter, you may need to make the dough in two batches. The amount of water needed may vary according to the type of processor and the kind of flour that is used. Once the dough is made, allow it to rest for twenty to thirty minutes, then continue kneading and rinsing as described in Steps 4–9 in the recipe for Traditional Homemade Gluten (pages 14–15).

STORING GLUTEN

Raw gluten can be refrigerated or frozen then cooked at a later time. Gluten becomes even more elastic after it has been chilled for a few hours, which is especially useful for dishes that require stretching or shaping of the uncooked gluten. As gluten stores very well, it is possible to prepare batches in advance.

To refrigerate gluten, place it in a container and add water to cover. Cover tightly and refrigerate for up to one week. To maintain maximum freshness, change the water every two days. When you are ready to cook the gluten, remove it from the container and rinse it off under cold running water, squeezing it firmly a few times.

Stored in the freezer, gluten will keep for up to six weeks. To freeze, place the gluten in a zipper-style freezer bag (two cups of gluten will fit into one sandwich-size bag of this type). Press the excess air from the bag and seal. Freeze the bag on a baking tray or other smooth, flat surface. (Frozen this way, many bags of gluten can be stacked in the freezer and will use a minimal amount of space.)

To defrost the frozen gluten quickly, simply place the bag in a large bowl or saucepan. Open the bag (leaving the frozen gluten inside), and fill the bowl with very hot water. After ten minutes, replace the water with more hot water. Within another ten minutes, the gluten should be thawed and ready to cook.

If you are freezing gluten that has been formed into cutlet shapes, layer the cutlets between sheets of plastic wrap. Stack three to six cutlets, wrap the stack in aluminum foil, and freeze. To defrost, remove the stack from the foil and separate the cutlets. Left at room temperature, the gluten will be defrosted and ready to cook in a few hours.

Ϩ About Herbs

Unless otherwise noted, dried herbs are to be used for the recipes in this book. Of course, feel free to use fresh herbs if you prefer. You must keep in mind, however, that the equivalent amount of dried to fresh herbs varies. As a general rule, 1 tablespoon of a fresh herb is equivalent to 1 teaspoon dried.

Use the following quick-reference chart for figuring fresh-to-dried herb equivalents:

FRESH		DRIED
1 tsp.	=	⅓ tsp.
2 tsp.	=	⅔ tsp.
1 tbsp.	=	1 tsp.
2 tbsp.	=	2 tsp.
3 tbsp.	=	1 tbsp.
¼ cup	=	4 tsp.
½ cup	=	2 tbsp.

FLAVORING SEITAN

When we began cooking with seitan in 1971, the only flavoring we used was a combination of fresh ginger, soy sauce, kombu, and water. This ingredient combination continues to be the traditional cooking broth for flavoring seitan. The soy sauce and kombu give seitan a rich dark brown color and hearty, salty flavor, and provide an excellent base for building more complex flavors.

Over the years, our culinary experiences grew and we became familiar with a wide array of exotic and delightfully flavored international dishes. Our desire to translate some of these exciting flavors to "seitan cuisine" grew as well. This urge inspired us to embark on a cooking adventure in which we used different combinations of herbs and spices to add unique and "new" flavors to seitan.

Our efforts resulted in the creation of four exceptional seasoning blends—aromatic, savory, spicy, and hearty (page 21). Many of the recipes in this book call for these herb-and-spice combinations. Using the seasoning blends will increase the variety of tastes you can achieve with seitan and, hopefully, inspire you to create your own flavor combinations. The traditional Basic Broth recipe that follows is for simmering 2 to 2½ cups (1¼ to 1½ pounds) of gluten. Also, any one of the special seasoning blends can be added to the Basic Broth for additional flavor to the gluten as it simmers. (Omit the ginger from the Basic Broth if you are adding a seasoning blend.)

BASIC BROTH

A flavorful broth in which to simmer 2 to 2$\frac{1}{2}$ cups of gluten.

4 cups water
¼–½ cup natural soy sauce (use ½ cup for stronger flavor)
3-inch piece kombu
4–6 slices (⅛ inch) fresh ginger root (optional)
1 tablespoon sesame oil (optional)

• *If a less salty or unsalted seitan is required, omit part or all of the soy sauce and use only the kombu and a few slices of ginger.*

THE SPECIAL SEASONING BLENDS

Following are the herb-and-spice combinations for the special seasoning blends. In addition to combining one of the blends with the Basic Broth (above), mixing a blend with ground seitan makes tastier burgers and loaves. The seasoning blends can also be added to sauces, marinades, breadings, and batters.

Please note, all the ingredients called for in the following blends are in their dried form.

Aromatic Blend

1 teaspoon sesame seeds
¾ teaspoon ground coriander
¾ teaspoon cumin
½ teaspoon garlic granules
½ teaspoon onion flakes
¼ teaspoon celery seeds
⅛ teaspoon white pepper

Hearty Blend

4 teaspoons paprika
4 teaspoons parsley
1 teaspoon basil
1 teaspoon celery seeds
¾ teaspoon garlic granules
  or powder
½ teaspoon sage
¼ teaspoon rosemary
¼ teaspoon white pepper

Spicy Blend

1½ teaspoons garlic granules
1½ teaspoons oregano
1 teaspoon paprika
¾ teaspoon fennel
½ teaspoon dry mustard
½ teaspoon sage
⅜ teaspoon black pepper
⅜ teaspoon white pepper

Savory Blend

2 tablespoons parsley flakes
2 teaspoons tarragon
1¼ teaspoons garlic granules
1 teaspoon dill
1 teaspoon fenugreek
1 teaspoon onion flakes
¾ teaspoon celery seeds
½ teaspoon thyme
¼ teaspoon sage

STEP 2 COOKING THE GLUTEN

Unless you are refrigerating or freezing your freshly made gluten, it is time for the second step in the seitan-making process—cooking the gluten. By using different types of gluten, seasonings, and cooking methods, you can create seitan with a wide variety of textures and flavors. The following cooking techniques—pan-simmering, oven-braising, pressure-cooking, baking, and deep-frying—give you a variety of choices for transforming gluten into seitan.

PAN-SIMMERED GLUTEN

Slowly pan-simmering raw gluten in a seasoned broth is the easiest, most basic method for making seitan. When cooked, the gluten will be nearly doubled in size. For every 2 to 2½ cups of gluten (formed into cutlets, cubes, or strips) use 1 recipe of Basic Broth (page 20). Adding a seasoning blend (above) to the broth is, of course, optional.
  Follow these steps when pan-simmering:

1. In a 4- or 5-quart saucepan or stockpot, bring the Basic Broth and seasoning blend (if using) to a low boil. Reduce the heat and add the gluten, a few pieces at a time (if simmering cutlets, add them one at a time).
2. Partially cover the pot and simmer the gluten. Very few bubbles should be evident in the simmering broth. (Do not let the broth boil, as this will result in seitan that is too soft and spongy). Rearrange the pieces occasionally to ensure even penetration of the seasonings.
3. Simmer the gluten for about 2 hours, or until most of the broth has been absorbed. Remove the pot from the heat and let the seitan remain in the broth until it cools to room temperature. (The pieces will become more firm as they cool, making them easier to remove without breaking.)
4. The seitan is now ready to be eaten as is. It can also be pan-fried, deep-fried, braised, broiled, or ground.

Variation

"Very Thin" Cutlets

If gluten has been pressed into very thin cutlets and simmered in broth, the result will be seitan cutlets that are extremely firm. When these cutlets are then pan-fried, deep-fried, or braised in sauce, they will become tender. We prefer this basic preparation because it results in seitan cutlets that are adaptable to many styles of cooking.

Follow the same basic guidelines just described for pan-simmering gluten, but keep in mind that it is critical to maintain a *very low* heat throughout the simmering. Using higher heat will result in softer seitan.

1. Add the gluten pieces to the broth one at a time. Hold one of the flattened cutlets at both ends and lay it on top of the hot broth. Using a flat wooden spoon or spatula, push the cutlet below the surface of the broth before adding the next piece of gluten.
2. Simmer the cutlets in an uncovered or partially covered pot. Occasionally, you should gently reposition the cutlets to ensure even penetration of the seasonings.
3. Allow the cutlets to simmer for about 1–1 ½ hours, or until they absorb most of the broth. (Refrigerate any remaining broth and reserve it for use in soups, sauces, and stews.) Remove the pot from the heat and let the seitan pieces remain in the broth until they cool to room temperature. (The cutlets will become firm as

Save That Starch Water!

Starch water refers to the combination of water, starch, and bran that remains after extracting gluten from wheat flour. After pouring off this starch water, set it aside for $2^1/_2$ hours. During this time, the starch water will separate. The thin, light-colored "clear" water will rise to the top, while the thick water settles on the bottom.

CLEAR STARCH WATER

Once the starch water separates, pour the thin, clear starch water into a separate container. Use it in the following ways:

- *Add it to bath water; it is a wonderful skin moisturizer.*
- *Mix a small amount with regular water and use it to water plants.*
- *Give it to pets as part of their daily liquid.*

Tightly covered and refrigerated, this clear starch water will keep up to one week.

THICK STARCH WATER

This nutrient-rich byproduct of homemade gluten is an excellent thickening agent. Use it in the following ways:

- *As a thickener for soups and stews, sauces and gravies, and some desserts.*
- *To make sourdough starter for bread (see page 26).*

Before storing the thick starch water, add a 1-inch layer of fresh water, but do not mix them together. Cover the container and refrigerate. Every two or three days, carefully pour off this water and replace it with fresh water. To use the thick starch, simply pour off the water, scoop out the amount of starch needed, and add another layer of fresh water. Any water that is accidentally mixed with the starch will separate to the top within an hour.

Covered tightly and refrigerated, this thick starch will keep from four to six days. If the starch begins to bubble, you can use it to make sourdough starter.

Another method of preserving the thick starch from the water is to dry it. Pour the thick starch onto a clean baking sheet and spread it out evenly to no more than a $^1/_{16}$-inch thickness. (Use extra

sheets if necessary.) Set the sheet away from the general kitchen traffic in a dry place where there is plenty of air circulating (or the starch will turn moldy). When the starch is dry to the touch, break it into 2-inch pieces to quicken the drying time. Once the starch is completely dry (it may take a few days), pulverize it in the blender and store in a covered container. As long as the starch is thoroughly dry, it will not require refrigeration. Reconstituted with water, this dry wheat starch can be used in approximately the same proportions as arrowroot or kuzu.

they cool, making them easier to remove without breaking.) If you want to quickly chill the cutlets for use in a specific dish, carefully transfer them to a plate and place them in the refrigerator or freezer for 5–10 minutes.

4. The seitan cutlets are now ready to eat. They can also be pan-fried, deep-fried, braised, broiled, or ground.

OVEN-BRAISED GLUTEN

Like pan-simmering, oven-braising is an easy method for cooking gluten. For every 2 to 2½ cups of gluten (formed into cutlets or cubes) use 1 recipe of Basic Broth (page 20). A flameproof casserole dish or a Dutch oven is required.

1. Preheat the oven to 375°F.
2. In a 4- or 5-quart Dutch oven or flameproof casserole, bring the Basic Broth and seasoning blend (if using) to a low boil. Reduce the heat and add a few gluten pieces at a time. Cover the pot or casserole dish and transfer to the oven.
3. Every 20 minutes, turn over and rearrange the gluten/seitan pieces to ensure even seasoning.
4. After 1 hour, remove the cover and continue to braise the seitan, basting it frequently, until the liquid has been reduced to about ½ cup.
5. Remove the pot from the oven, and allow the seitan to cool in the remaining broth.
6. The seitan is now ready to eat. It can also be pan-fried, deep-fried, braised, broiled, or ground.

PRESSURE-COOKED GLUTEN

Pressure-cooking can be the answer when you want to make a one-dish, hearty meal in a short time. By combining pressure-cooked gluten with a few vegetables and using a little starch water as a thickener, you can create a nearly instant stew. The high heat and pressure will produce a softer-textured seitan. And, because the cooking time is shorter, there will be somewhat less penetration of the seasonings into the seitan.

The following steps describe the procedure for pressure-cooking gluten. For every 2 to 2½ cups of gluten (preferably cut or broken into chunks the size of ping-pong balls), use 1 recipe of Basic Broth (page 20). Add a seasoning blend (page 21) to the broth, if you desire.

1. In a pressure cooker, bring the broth to a boil, then slowly add the gluten pieces. Cover and seal the pressure cooker and raise the heat. When the cooker comes to pressure, reduce the heat to a simmer and cook the gluten about 20 minutes.
2. Reduce the pressure by placing the pot in the sink and running cool water over the top. Do not open the cover until all pressure has been released.
3. Allow the seitan to cool in the broth for 20–30 minutes. It will become firmer as it cools.
4. The seitan can be simmered in sauce or gravy, added to soup, or used in a stew (see recipe for Quick Stew on page 71).

BAKED GLUTEN

Baking is an excellent method for cooking gluten that has been shaped into cutlets. The result is a food that can then be ground, simmered in sauce, or transformed into fillable pouches. Baked cutlets have a dry consistency, and are a good choice for making ground seitan.

For cutlets that will eventually be made into fillable pouches, use gluten made from unbleached white flour only. If the cutlets are to be ground once they are baked, use gluten that has been made either from unbleached white flour only or a combination of unbleached white and gluten flour.

The following steps describe the simple method for baking gluten:

1. Preheat the oven to 400°F. Lightly coat a baking sheet with vegetable oil.

Making Sourdough Starter

The thick starch water that comes from making gluten is excellent for making sourdough starter to use in your favorite sourdough bread recipe.

1. *After the reserved starch water from making gluten has separated into thick and clear starch waters, pour off about $^2/_3$ of the clear water. Mix the remaining clear water with the thick starch water.*

2. *Pour this batter into a glass jar or crock. Cover the container with a bamboo mat or clean cloth, and let it rest in a warm place with circulating air.*

3. *After about ten hours, and every three hours after that, stir the starter and check its development. The warmer and more humid the environment, the faster the fermentation will occur.*

4. *In one or two days the starter should be ready. It will have a thick-batter consistency, a slightly alcoholic yet sweet smell, and it will be filled with bubbles. As directed, use the batter in your favorite sourdough bread recipe.*

5. *If you do not use the starter at this point, store it, tightly wrapped, in the refrigerator. After one week, the starter should either be used or fed to keep it active. To feed the starter, simply mix in $^1/_2$ cup each of flour and water. Let the starter sit outside the refrigerator for a few hours, and stir it occasionally. The older a starter gets, the better it becomes, so it is worthwhile to keep it going.*

6. *Every time you use some of the starter, replace it with more flour and water. For instance, if you use 1 cup of the starter, add $^1/_2$ cup flour and $^1/_2$ cup water to replace what you have used. Allow the starter to sit in a warm place for a few hours before storing it, tightly covered, in the refrigerator.*

2. Form the gluten into a cylinder (about 3–4 inches in diameter), then slice it into ½-inch-thick cutlets. Arrange the cutlets on the baking sheet.
3. Bake the cutlets about 10 minutes before turning them over. Lightly brush more oil on the sheet before replacing the slices. Bake the cutlets until they are no longer sticky in the center (another 15 minutes).
4. The seitan cutlets are now ready to be ground, simmered, or formed into pouches. (See the following variations).

Variation 1

Seitan Pouches

Filled with leftover grains and vegetables, seitan pouches are perfect fare to include in a picnic basket or bag lunch. Crowned with a sauce, filled seitan pouches also make an elegant entrée.

1. Form a pouch by cutting the seitan cutlet in half crosswise. Fill the pouch with cooked vegetables, grains, or your favorite pâté.
2. After filling the pouch, pinch the edges together and secure with a toothpick or two (as if sewing the pouch shut).
3. Place the pouches in a steamer that has been set over ½ inch of boiling water. Steam for 5 minutes.

Variation 2

Ground Seitan

A very light-textured seitan comes from gluten that has been baked. (Pan-simmered or oven-braised gluten is also good for making ground seitan.) Used to make croquettes, patties, loaves, and burgers, ground seitan can also be added to casseroles, tossed into salads, or used as a garnish for soups. Some natural foods stores carry frozen ground seitan.

1. Cut baked seitan cutlets into small pieces.
2. Add the pieces to a blender or food processor and process until the seitan becomes coarse and crumbly (do not over-process).
3. The ground seitan is now ready to use.

Variation 3

Twice-Baked Cutlets

1. Pan-simmer baked seitan cutlets in Basic Broth (page 20) or other seasoned stock for 15 minutes.
2. Carefully remove the cutlets from the broth, place them on a plate, and allow them to cool at room temperature for 15 minutes. (For faster cooling, place the hot cutlets in the refrigerator or freezer.)
3. Place the cooled cutlets on an oiled baking sheet and place in a 400°F oven. Bake the cutlets for 10 minutes on each side. (You can opt to broil the cutlets for about 4 minutes on each side.) If you desire, brush the cutlets with a little oil and sprinkle with your choice of seasonings before baking.
4. Served warm or cold, these cutlets are wonderful in sandwiches. They can also be cut into cubes or strips and added to salads and vegetable dishes.

DEEP-FRIED GLUTEN

Figure 2.7
Filtering used oil.

Deep-frying gluten is a useful method for a variety of dishes, producing seitan that ranges in texture from crisp and chewy to smooth and tender. Deep-frying gluten before simmering it in a seasoned broth results in a rich-flavored seitan that is very different in taste and texture from that of plain simmered seitan.

Deep-frying can be a healthful, easy cooking method if you follow a few simple guidelines. Choosing the right oil and cooking pot should be your first important consideration. We have found sunflower, canola, and peanut oil (or a combination of these oils) to be the best for deep-frying. Unrefined corn oil is not recommended because it foams as it heats.

It is best to use fresh oil (ideally, the same oil should not be used more than twice) for deep-frying, and it should never be heated to the point of smoking. If the oil becomes very dark, it should be discarded. One method of preserving used oil is to strain it. Place a sheet of strong paper towel or a double layer of cheesecloth over the mouth of a clean glass or plastic container. Allow the center of the towel to extend about two inches into the container. Secure the towel to the container with a rubber band. Slowly pour the used oil over the towel, letting it filter into the container (Figure 2.7). Remove and discard the towel. Cover the container of oil and refrigerate.

A three- or four-quart stainless steel saucepan is a good basic utensil for deep-frying; however, some people prefer to use a wok. A cast iron pot is not recommended because it retains heat so well that regulating the oil temperature is difficult. This can result in food that is either overcooked or undercooked.

Good organization is an integral part of successful deep-frying. Make sure all ingredients are ready before you heat the oil. Have on hand a baking sheet with three or four layers of paper towel on which to place the hot cooked seitan.

The correct oil temperature is critical to successfully deep-fry gluten or seitan. Drop a tiny piece of gluten/seitan into the heated oil. If the piece does not rise to the top, but rather remains on the bottom of the pan, the oil is too cool. Food cooked in this oil will be damp, soggy, and saturated with oil. You will know the oil is too hot if it smokes, or if the piece of gluten stays on top and spins or moves around rapidly. Food cooked in this oil will be overcooked on the outside and raw on the inside.

The temperature of the oil is correct if the gluten sinks to the bottom of the pan then immediately rises to the top and spins gently while surrounded by tiny bubbles. Food that is properly deep-fried will be crispy (not burned or soggy) on the outside and tender (not raw or wet) on the inside. Any excess oil will be absorbed by the paper towels.

When deep-frying gluten, follow the steps presented below. (Never use batter when deep-frying raw gluten. However, batter can be used with cooked gluten/seitan.)

1. Squeeze the gluten firmly to remove any excess water. If necessary, pat the gluten lightly with a paper or cloth towel.
2. Heat 2–4 inches of oil in a 3-quart saucepan or a wok that has been set over medium–high heat. When the oil is ready (as previously instructed) carefully lower one piece of gluten into the pan.
3. Using a pair of chopsticks or long forks, hold the piece of gluten under the oil for about 1 minute. The gluten will puff up dramatically in all directions but will deflate somewhat as it cools. Cook the gluten in the hot oil 1–1½ minutes, then turn the piece over and cook it another minute or so until it is golden brown. Place on absorbent paper towels to remove any excess oil. Repeat with the remaining gluten.
4. The seitan should be crisp on the outside and somewhat moist (not wet or dry) on the inside.

Variation

Deep-Frying Seitan

Once gluten has been pan-simmered or oven-braised in a seasoned broth, the cooked seitan can then be deep-fried. Coating the cooked pieces with a tasty batter before deep-frying adds another interesting dimension to this food. (For information on batter and batter recipes, see When Using Batter on page 31.)

STORING SEITAN

Whenever I prepare seitan for our family, I make more than I need for just one meal. Leftover seitan is a great sandwich filler, a hearty casserole ingredient, and a delicious snack food. Like gluten, seitan can be refrigerated or frozen. Slow-simmered seitan and its cooking broth can be stored in a tightly sealed container and refrigerated for up to ten days.

Salt, which is a preservative, is one reason why commercially prepared seitan is usually very salty. Some brands claim to have a shelf-life of one month; but, in order to have such a long shelf life, the seitan must be stored at a temperature of 33°F. Generally, home refrigerators are not that cold (most average a temperature of 45°F). Seitan that is mild-flavored and only slightly salty can be refrigerated for three to six days.

Plastic freezer containers and zipper-style freezer bags can be used to store all types of seitan. The seitan should be at room temperature or chilled before freezing.

To freeze cutlets, individually wrap them in plastic wrap. Stack three to six cutlets, wrap them together in aluminum foil, and freeze. To defrost, remove the foil and separate the cutlets. In most recipes, the seitan cutlets should be defrosted before they are used.

Baked, ground seitan can be frozen without special preparation. Simply place the ground seitan in a plastic container or freezer bag. Ground seitan defrosts very quickly at room temperature. Deep-fried seitan (uncoated) and most prepared seitan dishes (cutlets in sauce, "sausages," burgers, etc.) also adapt very well to freezing.

When Using Batter

Deep-frying seitan that has been coated with a delicious seasoned batter is a tasty option. If using batter, keep the following tips in mind:

- *Chill the batter for a crisper coating.*
- *Before coating the seitan, be sure to remove any excess moisture. If necessary, blot the seitan gently with a paper towel.*

- *Don't overcrowd the pot. The coated pieces of seitan should not touch (there should be at least a half-inch space between them). Cook one or two cutlets at a time (or five to eight cubes, depending on their size).*

Each of the following batter recipes will coat approximately five to ten seitan cutlets (depending on their size and thickness).

WHOLE WHEAT AND CORN FLOUR BATTER

1 cup whole wheat pastry flour
½ cup corn flour
1 teaspoon sea salt
1 tablespoon arrowroot flour
1¼ cups water

Blend all the dry ingredients well with a fork. Mix in the water. Refrigerate the batter at least 10 minutes before using.

WHOLE WHEAT BATTER

1⅓ cups whole wheat pastry flour
1¼ cups water
½ teaspoon sea salt

Combine all the ingredients well with a fork, Refrigerate the batter at least 10 minutes before using.

SEASONED BATTER

1½ cups whole wheat pastry flour
3 tablespoons arrowroot flour
2 tablespoons seasoning blend of choice
1½ cups water

Blend all the dry ingredients with a fork. Add the water and mix well—a few lumps will not be a problem. Refrigerate at least 10 minutes before using.

A FINAL WORD

Now that you know how to make your own gluten and seitan, you can embark on the second stage of this culinary adventure. The recipes in this book have been developed especially with homemade seitan in mind, but you can use the commercially made product (available in natural foods stores) with equally successful results.

The inspiration for these recipes has come from different cultures and ethnic culinary traditions. Whether you try your hand at a simple seitan dish or more elaborate preparation, you will find cooking with seitan a unique, healthful, and most enjoyable experience.

3
APPETIZERS AND SNACKS

*Strange to see how a good dinner and feasting
reconciles everybody.*

—Samuel Pepys (1633–1703)
Diary

The seitan dishes presented in this chapter are perfect
to enjoy as snacks, side dishes, or preludes to a
meal. From Savory Nuggets (page 34) to Dolmadakia—
Stuffed Grape Leaves (page 36) to Dim Sum Wontons
(page 49), you will find a variety of cooking styles and
flavors—enough to satisfy a wide range of appetites.

Some of the dishes in this chapter are quick to
prepare, others are more involved; some are better
served hot, others cold. You might prepare a buffet
and include a number of these delectable seitan treats.

Whether you serve the dishes as appetizers, snacks,
or as part of a larger meal, you will discover all of them
to be delicious and enjoyable to prepare. I encourage
you to be creative and use these recipe ideas as starting
points for your own combinations of cooking styles and
flavorings.

SAVORY NUGGETS

CALLS FOR:
Seitan pieces

SUGGESTED
COOKING METHOD:
Deep-frying

YIELD:
4–6 servings

Quick to prepare, these crispy, seasoned nuggets can be served as an appetizer or side dish. Delicious plain, they can also be accompanied by a dip or sauce. Feel free to substitute the suggested seasonings with the seasonings of your choice.

2 cups (about 1 pound) seitan pieces (1 x 2 inches)
Oil for deep-frying
1 egg
¼ cup plain soymilk or Rice Dream Beverage
1 cup cornmeal
2 tablespoons arrowroot flour
1 recipe Savory Seasoning Blend (page 21)

1. Pat the seitan pieces dry with absorbent paper towels and set aside.
2. In a medium bowl, beat together the egg and soymilk. In another bowl, combine the cornmeal, arrowroot, and Savory Seasoning Blend.
3. Heat 2–3 inches of oil in a 3- or 4-quart saucepan.
4. While the oil is heating, dip the seitan pieces into the egg mixture, then coat the pieces with the seasoned cornmeal. Repeat this procedure, so the seitan pieces are dipped twice into the egg and cornmeal.
5. Without overcrowding the pan, carefully deep-fry the seitan in small batches until golden brown and crispy (5–8 minutes). Place on absorbent paper towels to remove any excess oil.
6. Arrange the hot nuggets on a platter and serve them plain or with your choice of dipping sauce. (For a wide range of sauce suggestions, see Chapter 4, beginning on page 53).

Variations

Try serving Savory Nuggets in the following ways:

• Add to steamed vegetables and serve with a salad dressing.

- Add to stir-fried vegetables.
- Garnish a thick puréed soup.

QUICK AND TANGY SEITAN CUBES

Try these quick and easy cubes as a hearty appetizer. For a sandwich filling, use slices instead of cubes.

2 cups (about 1 pound) seitan cubes (1 inch)
Oil for deep-frying
1 recipe Tangy Mustard Sauce (page 58)
1 scallion, sliced thin

CALLS FOR:
Seitan cubes

SUGGESTED
COOKING METHODS:
Deep-frying,
then pan-simmering

YIELD:
4–6 servings

1. Heat 2–3 inches of oil in a 3- or 4-quart saucepan. Without overcrowding the pan, deep-fry the seitan cubes in small batches until they are crispy on all sides (about 5 minutes).* Place on absorbent paper towels to remove any excess oil.
2. In a 1- or 2-quart saucepan, heat the Tangy Mustard Sauce then add the seitan. Stir well and simmer the seitan until it is heated through (about 5 minutes). Remove from the heat and add most of the scallion, reserving some slices to use as a garnish.
3. Serve the cubes hot or cold as an appetizer, side dish, or sandwich filling.

* Instead of deep-frying the seitan, you can also broil it. Simply place the cubes on an oiled baking sheet and broil them until they are crispy on all sides.

DOLMADAKIA—
STUFFED GRAPE LEAVES

CALLS FOR:
Ground seitan

SUGGESTED
COOKING METHOD:
Pan-simmering

YIELD:
About 30 rolls
(1 x 3 inches)

Ambitious cooks will enjoy making and serving these delightful traditional Greek rolls as a savory appetizer or side dish. Although this dish is time-consuming to make, you can prepare it a day or two before serving it. Covered and refrigerated, dolmadakia keeps well for two or three days.

2 cups ground seitan (about 1 pound)
8-ounce jar grape leaves in brine
1 cup long-grain brown rice (uncooked)
2 cups warm water
1 recipe Hearty Seasoning Blend (page 21)
½ medium onion, chopped very fine
2 tablespoons paprika
¼ cup crushed dried mint leaves
¼ teaspoon black pepper
2 tablespoons natural soy sauce
3 cups boiling water (more, if necessary)
2 tablespoons olive oil for drizzling over rolls

SAUCE
1 tablespoon kuzu
Water (enough to measure 1¼ cups when added
to remaining broth)
3 tablespoons lemon juice

1. In a small bowl, soak the rice in the warm water for 2 hours. When the rice has almost finished soaking, remove the grape leaves from the jar and drain them. Place the leaves in a bowl of cold water for 15 minutes to remove some of the salt. Drain and repeat. Fill the bowl with water again. Gently unroll and separate the leaves as they sit in the water. (Be careful, they are quite delicate.) Transfer the leaves to a colander to drain.

2. To make the filling, place the seitan in a medium bowl. Add half the Hearty Seasoning Blend, the onion, paprika,

mint, black pepper, and soy sauce. Drain the rice and add it to the bowl. Mix all the ingredients together well.

3. Oil a deep skillet or heavy saucepan. Line the bottom of the pan with a few grape leaves. Set aside.

4. Place a grape leaf on your work surface vein-side up with the stem pointing toward you. Place 2 tablespoons of the filling in the center of the leaf near the stem end. Starting at the stem end, roll up the leaf, folding the left and right sides of the leaf snugly over the filling. Place the roll seam side down in the leaf-lined skillet. Repeat with the remaining leaves and filling.

5. When all the rolls have been assembled, drizzle them with olive oil. Combine the remaining seasoning blend with the boiling water and pour it over the rolls (this broth should just reach the top of the rolls). Cover the rolls with a layer of 4 or 5 flat grape leaves.

6. Place a plate on top of the rolls to keep them from unrolling as they cook. Bring the broth to a boil, then immediately reduce the heat. Simmer the rolls for 1¼ hours.

7. Remove the cover and allow the rolls to cool to room temperature in the pot, or carefully transfer them to a platter. Reserve any remaining broth.

8. To make the sauce, measure 1¼ cups of the cool reserved broth. Add water as needed to attain this measurement. Dissolve the kuzu in ¼ cup of the broth and set aside. In a small saucepan, bring the remaining broth to a low boil and add the lemon juice. Add the kuzu while stirring constantly until the sauce thickens to a syrupy consistency. If the sauce is too thick, add a little water while stirring. Adjust the seasonings as needed.

9. To serve, place the hot or cold dolmadakia on a platter and spoon the sauce over the top.

MARINATED SEITAN BITS

CALLS FOR:
Gluten

SUGGESTED
COOKING METHOD:
Broiling

YIELD:
Depends on
amount of gluten

This quick method of marinating then broiling gluten is perfect for using up leftover pieces. Try these bits with Tangy Mustard Sauce (page 58), your favorite salad dressing, or any of the barbecue-sauce variations found in Chapter 4.

Gluten pieces (½–1 inch)
Enough sauce or dressing (of choice) to cover gluten pieces

1. Place the gluten pieces in a bowl and completely cover them with sauce or dressing. Marinate the pieces for 15 minutes.
2. Arrange the the gluten on an oiled baking sheet and place under the broiler (about 6 inches from the heat source). Broil 1–2 minutes on each side.
3. Serve seitan bits hot or at room temperature, as an addition to cooked vegetables or salads, or as a garnish for soups.

PEPPERONI JERKY CHIPS

CALLS FOR:
Seitan sausage

SUGGESTED
COOKING METHOD:
Deep-frying

YIELD:
Approximately 2 cups

These crispy chips are a great snack. They also add a spicy spark to salads and soups.

1 recipe plain or hickory-flavored Spicy Seitan Sausage
(page 126)
Oil for deep-frying

1. Slice the seitan sausage into ⅛-inch-thick rounds and set aside.
2. Heat 2–3 inches of oil in a 3- or 4-quart saucepan. Without overcrowding the pan, add the seitan slices in small batches and deep-fry them until crispy (1–3 minutes).* Place on absorbent paper towels to remove any excess oil.
3. Enjoy these chips as a snack, or use them as a garnish for soups, salads, or cooked vegetables.

* Instead of deep-frying the chips, you can also broil them. Simply place the slices on an oiled baking sheet and broil them about 3 minutes on each side.

DILLED NUGGETS IN VELVET DILL SAUCE

CALLS FOR:
Homemade gluten

SUGGESTED
COOKING METHODS:
Deep-frying, then
pan-simmering

YIELD:
4 servings

Velvet Dill Sauce is perfect for blanketing these crisp, succulent nuggets. Tangy Mustard Sauce (page 58) is another good sauce choice.

1 cup gluten flour
4 tablespoons dehydrated vegetable broth mix*
(if mix contains salt, use 2 tablespoons only)
3 tablespoons dried dill, or ½ cup minced fresh
1 cup water
Oil for deep-frying

VELVET DILL SAUCE
1½ cups plain soymilk or Rice Dream beverage
1 tablespoon kuzu
¼ cup water
2 tablespoons dry white wine or sake
2–3 tablespoons finely chopped fresh dill

* Available in natural foods stores and supermarkets.

1. In a medium bowl, blend the flour and vegetable broth mix together. Mix in the dill. Make a well in the center of the flour mixture, add the water, and mix the ingredients vigorously with a fork to form a soft dough. Form the dough into a ball and let it rest 10–20 minutes.
2. Heat 2–3 inches of oil in a 3- or 4-quart saucepan.
3. Pull off bite-size pieces of gluten from the ball of dough. Without overcrowding pot, add the pieces in small batches and deep-fry them until crispy on all sides (4–8 minutes). Place on absorbent paper towels to remove any excess oil.
4. To make the Velvet Dill Sauce, heat the soymilk in a 1-quart saucepan. Add the deep-fried seitan and simmer about 20 minutes, stirring occasionally.
5. While the seitan is simmering, dissolve the kuzu in the water then add it to the pan. Stir until the sauce is creamy. Add the wine and dill, and simmer 10 minutes more.

6. Add the nuggets to the hot sauce and heat together 3–5 minutes. Serve warm.

CALLS FOR:
Gluten

SUGGESTED
COOKING METHOD:
Deep-frying

YIELD:
About 24 spirals

GREEN AND GOLDEN SPIRALS

Swiss chard or other dark leafy green vegetable is combined with gluten in this unusual presentation.

1 cup gluten
4 Swiss chard, bok choy, or spinach leaves (4 x 4 inches)
Oil for deep-frying
1 recipe Tangy Mustard Sauce (page 58) for dipping

1. Wash the leaves and pat them dry. Remove the stems (including any part of the stem that extends into the leaf).
2. Divide the gluten into 4 equal pieces. Working with one piece at a time, place the gluten on your work surface and carefully stretch it into a 4-x-4-inch shape. Hold the stretched gluten flat with the palm of one hand (or it will immediately curl up) and place one of the leaves on top.
3. Immediately roll the gluten into a tight cylinder. As you roll it, tuck in any pieces of the protruding leaf. Press the edges together and place the cylinder seam side down on a plate. Repeat with the remaining leaves and gluten.
4. Heat 2–3 inches of oil in a 3- or 4-quart saucepan.
5. Deep-fry the rolls, one by one, until they are bubbly and golden (3–5 minutes). Place the rolls on absorbent paper towels to remove any excess oil.
6. Slice each roll into ½-inch rounds (6 to 8 rounds per roll).
7. Without overcrowding the pan, add the slices in small batches and deep-fry them again. This time the inside section of the spiral will puff up. Turn the piece over a few times to ensure even cooking. Cook the spirals until they are crispy and golden, then place them on absorbent paper towels to remove any excess oil.
8. Serve warm with Tangy Mustard Sauce.

CORN DOGGIES

CALLS FOR:
Seitan cubes

SUGGESTED
COOKING METHOD:
Deep-frying

YIELD:
About 20 pieces

These tender yet crispy morsels are our tribute to the famous tan pups (see page 3 for the story). Quick to prepare, Corn Doggies are a favorite with snackers of all ages. Serve them plain or with a dipping sauce. We enjoy them best with Salsa Picante (page 60).

20 seitan cubes, 1½ x 2 inches (about 1 pound)
Oil for deep-frying
1 cup cornmeal

BATTER
¾ cup whole wheat pastry flour plus ¼ cup corn flour
(or 1 cup pastry flour)
1 tablespoon minced fresh parsley, or 1 teaspoon dried
2–3 teaspoons seasoning blend of choice, page 21
(or ½ teaspoon sea salt, 2 teaspoons onion flakes,
and 2 teaspoons garlic flakes or granules)
½ teaspoon coarsely ground black pepper
2 tablespoons arrowroot flour
1 medium egg, optional*
½ cup water

* If omitting the egg, increase the water to ¾ cup.

1. Pat the seitan cubes dry with an absorbent paper towel. Place the cornmeal in a medium bowl and set aside.
2. In another medium bowl, combine all the batter ingredients and mix them together until smooth (if too thick, add a little more water). Allow the batter to rest for 10 minutes.
3. Heat 2–3 inches of oil in a 3- or 4-quart saucepan.
4. While the oil is heating, dip the seitan pieces (one at a time) into the batter. Gently shake the excess batter back into the bowl, then immediately roll the coated seitan in the cornmeal.
5. Without overcrowding the pot, add the seitan in small batches and deep-fry it until crispy and golden (4–7 minutes). Place on absorbent paper towels to remove any excess oil.

6. Arrange the corn doggies on a serving dish and enjoy them plain or with you favorite dipping sauce.

MINI-CROQUETTES

CALLS FOR:
Ground seitan

SUGGESTED
COOKING METHODS:
Deep-frying or baking

YIELD:
About 20 croquettes
(1-inch diameter)

These small croquettes add a crunchy, chewy accent to soups, salads, and steamed vegetables. Served with your favorite dip, they are also a great snack.

2 cups chilled ground seitan (about 1–1¼ pounds)
¼ cup chickpea flour
2 tablespoons whole wheat pastry flour
1 recipe seasoning blend of choice (page 21), optional
2 tablespoons sesame, corn, or olive oil
(if baking croquettes), or enough oil for deep-frying

1. In a medium bowl, combine the seitan, chickpea flour, pastry flour, and seasoning blend (if using). If baking the croquettes, add the oil to the ingredients and combine well. (Do not add oil to the mixture if you will be deep-frying the croquettes.)
2. Form the seitan mixture into 1-inch balls.
3. If deep-frying, heat 2–3 inches of oil in a 3- or 4-quart saucepan. Without overcrowding the pan (allowing at least 1 inch between the croquettes), cook the seitan until crispy and golden. Place on absorbent paper towels to remove any excess oil.
4. If baking the croquettes, preheat the oven to 350°F. Place the croquettes on a lightly oiled baking sheet and bake them until browned and firm (about 20 minutes).
5. Enjoy these croquettes as a tasty addition to salads and vegetable dishes, or as a garnish for soups. As an hors d'oeuvre, they are wonderful when served alongside a dip or blanketed in a favorite sauce. Chickpea Gravy (page 61) is an ideal accompaniment.

ఎ **About Oils**

Unrefined olive, corn, safflower, and sesame oils, as well as canola, peanut, and sunflower oils are recommended for their superior cooking qualities and flavors. These oils are rich in monounsaturates or polyunsaturates, essential fatty acids, and other valuable nutrients.

FIVE-SPICE POUCHES WITH BROCCOLI

Glazed with a delicate, aromatic sauce, these versatile little pouches can be served as an appetizer or a side dish. Once filled, the pouches must be steamed, then deep-fried before they are heated in a sauce, but I'm sure you will find them well worth the extra effort.

CALLS FOR:
Gluten

SUGGESTED
COOKING METHODS:
Steaming, deep-frying,
then pan-simmering

YIELD:
12 filled pouches

1 cup gluten
1 cup broccoli flowerets
2 tablespoons chickpea flour
Oil for deep-frying

SAUCE
1 cup water
1½ tablespoons natural soy sauce
3 tablespoons unsweetened pineapple, in its own juice
1 teaspoon Chinese 5-spice powder
1 tablespoon thick starch from making homemade seitan,
(or 1 tablespoon arrowroot or kuzu)

To assemble the pouches:

1. First make the filling. Steam or parboil the broccoli for about 3 minutes, then refresh it in cold water. Drain, then mince the broccoli and place it in a bowl along with the chickpea flour. Combine well and set aside.

2. Next make the pouches. Divide the gluten into 4 equal pieces, then divide each piece into thirds. Let the pieces rest about 2 inches away from each other on a damp smooth surface. (A damp surface will prevent the gluten from sticking.)

3. Take a gluten piece and, with a rotating motion, press and flatten it with the palm and heel of your hand until it is a 3-inch square and very thin. Hold the square open with one hand, positioning it as a diamond with one corner pointing toward you.

4. Place 1 tablespoon of the filling about 1 inch away from one of the corners. While continuing to hold the gluten

open and flat, fold the corner nearest the filling up and over the filling. Next, fold the left and right corners over the filling, stretching them slightly while forming a tightly sealed package. Finally, pick up the last corner and, stretching it slightly, bring it up and over the top of the package. Don't be concerned if the wrapping seems to extend too far over the pouch—more layers of a thin, tight wrapping are better than a few layers that are thick and loose.

5. Place the filled pouch seam side down on a plate and continue to form the rest of the pouches. (These few minutes of setting time will help ensure a good seal on the edges.)

To cook the filled pouches:

1. Fill a 3- or 4-quart saucepan with about 1 inch of water. Place a steamer basket inside the pan. (If you are cooking a very large quantity of pouches, I recommend using a bamboo steamer set over a wok or large frying pan.)

2. Wet a clean, smooth-textured cloth, such as a linen dish-towel, and squeeze it well. Use this damp cloth to line the steamer, then bring the water to a boil.

3. When the water begins to boil, place the pouches seam side down on the cloth-lined steamer. Cover the pan and steam the pouches for 8–10 minutes. Remove the pouches carefully and let them cool on a plate. (At this point, the cooled pouches can be covered and refrigerated, then cooked at a later time.)

4. While the pouches are cooling, heat 2–3 inches of oil in a 3- or 4-quart saucepan. Gently lower the pouches (no more than 3 at a time) into the hot oil and cook them, turning once, until they are golden and crispy (2–3 minutes). When turned, the pouches might bounce back to the cooked side. In this case, you will have to hold the pouch down in order to cook the other side. Place the cooked pouches on absorbent paper towels to remove any excess oil. (At this point, the pouches may be loosely covered with a cloth, paper towel, or bamboo mat and kept at room temperature for a few hours.)

5. Next prepare the sauce. Bring the water, soy sauce, pine-apple, and 5-spice powder to a boil in a medium sauce-pan. Reduce the heat and immerse the pouches in the sauce. Simmer the pouches uncovered for about 10 minutes, turning them a few times.
6. Carefully remove the pouches with a slotted spoon and arrange them on a platter.
7. Add the thick starch to the remaining hot broth, and stir it constantly until thick and glossy. (If using arrowroot or kuzu instead of the starch water, dissolve it in ¼ cup of cooled broth before returning it to the pan.) Continue to simmer the sauce, stirring it occasionally, until it is reduced to about ¼ cup (about 20 minutes).
8. To serve, either spoon the sauce onto a platter and arrange the pouches on top, or spoon the sauce over the pouches. Decorate the dish with a colorful garnish such as watercress sprigs, orange slices, or red radish flowers.

Variations

The beauty of these pouches is that they can be packed with any of a wide variety of luscious fillings and glazed with a number of different sauces or coatings. Try any of the following suggestions, or be innovative and create your own.

- As an appetizer or side dish, try filling the pouches with savory ground seitan that has been flavored with one of the seasoning blends (page 21).
- For a dessert or sweet snack, fill the pouches with a mixture of ground dates and nuts. Once they are deep-fried, glaze the pouches with hot maple syrup. You can also roll the pouches in maple sugar or a natural granulated sweetener such as Sucanat or Fruitsource.

CALLS FOR:
Ground seitan

SUGGESTED
COOKING METHOD:
Deep-frying

YIELD:
12 tortillas

SEITAN BANDITO

These crispy corn tortillas, filled with seasoned ground seitan and tofu, are meant to be served with Red Chilies Marengo.

1¼ cups ground seitan (about ¾ pound)
8 ounces mashed firm tofu
1 tablespoon Dijon-style mustard
1 recipe Hearty or Spicy Seasoning Blend (page 21),
or seasonings of your choice
12 soft corn tortillas
Oil for deep-frying
1 recipe Red Chilies Marengo (page 62)

1. Combine the seitan, tofu, mustard, and seasonings in a medium bowl.
2. Heat 2–3 inches of oil in a 3- or 4-quart saucepan.
3. While the oil is heating, place 1½ tablespoons of the seitan mixture across the middle third of a tortilla. Allowing about 1 inch between the filling and the edge of the tortilla, shape the filling into a 1-x-3-inch rectangle (about ½ inch thick). Pack the filling down firmly.
4. Roll up the tortilla, tucking it tightly around the filling. Hold the "package" closed between your thumb and index finger. Using a pair of tongs or long chopsticks, lower the tortilla into the hot oil and hold it there for 10 seconds. After this time it should stay together without being held, and you can assemble the next roll. Be careful to maintain the correct oil temperature.
5. Remove the tortilla roll when it is crispy and golden (about 5 minutes), and stand it upright on absorbent paper towels to remove any excess oil.
6. Serve hot with Red Chilies Marengo.

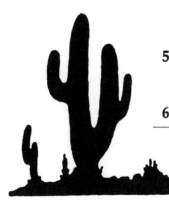

APRICOT-GLAZED FILO STRUDEL

CALLS FOR:
Ground seitan

SUGGESTED
COOKING METHOD:
Baking

YIELD:
4–6 servings

Before baking this delectable filo-wrapped strudel, glaze it with Apricot Sauce. Serve as an appetizer or side dish.

2 cups ground seitan (about 1 pound)
2 tablespoons chickpea flour
1 tablespoon Aromatic Seasoning Blend (page 21),
or seasoning of choice
4 filo leaves
½ cup unrefined corn oil, for brushing filo leaves

APRICOT SAUCE
3 tablespoons fruit-sweetened apricot jam
½ teaspoon unrefined corn oil
2 tablespoons water

1. Preheat the oven to 350°F. Lightly oil a 12-x-14-inch baking sheet and set aside.
2. To make the strudel filling, combine the seitan, flour, and Aromatic Seasoning Blend in a medium bowl. Set aside.
3. To form the glaze, blend the jam, oil, and water together well. Set aside.
4. Gently brush one of the filo leaves with oil. Place a second leaf on top of the first and brush it with oil. Repeat with the remaining leaves.
5. Arrange the filling in a 2-inch-thick narrow rectangle on the lower third of the dough, leaving a 2-inch border on the bottom edge (the edge closest to you), and a 1-inch border on each side. Fold the bottom edge of the filo over the filling, then fold in the left and right edges of the filo leaves. Roll up the filo to enclose the filling.
6. Carefully place the filled roll seam side down on a baking sheet. Top with half the Apricot Glaze and bake. After 20 minutes, brush the remaining glaze on top of the strudel and continue to bake for 10 minutes.
7. Allow the strudel to cool before slicing and serving.

HERBED SEITAN PÂTÉ

CALLS FOR:
Seitan

SUGGESTED COOKING METHOD:
Baking

YIELD:
About 2 cups

This favorful pâté is quick to assemble and takes only thirty minutes to bake. Serve it with your favorite crackers or vegetables, or use as a delicious sandwich filling.

2 cups seitan (about 1 pound)
2 cloves garlic
2 tablespoons chopped fresh parsley
2 teaspoons paprika
1 teaspoon thyme
1 teaspoon basil
½ teaspoon black pepper
3 tablespoons natural soy sauce
2 tablespoons olive oil
1 teaspoon lemon juice
2 tablespoons chickpea flour

1. Preheat the oven to 375°F.
2. In a blender or food processor, combine the seitan with all the remaining ingredients except the chickpea flour. Process until evenly ground but not mushy. Transfer the mixture to a bowl and add the chickpea flour. Mix together well.
3. Spoon the pâté mixture into one or two small, well-oiled oven-proof dishes. Bake 20–30 minutes.
4. Served warm or cool, this pâté is a sensational spread for bread or crackers.

DIM SUM WONTONS

CALLS FOR:
Ground seitan

SUGGESTED
COOKING METHOD:
Boiling

YIELD:
16 wontons

These easy-to-prepare filled wontons are great for a variety of occasions. Hot or chilled, with or without sauce, Dim Sum Wontons are perfect as appetizers, as well as brunch or lunch fare. Suggested sauces include sweet-and-sour, barbecue, dill, mustard, and citrus. (Sauce recipes are found in Chapter 4, beginning on page 53).

1 cup ground seitan (½–¾ pound)
1 recipe seasoning blend of choice (page 21)
16 square wonton wrappers,
or 4 egg roll wrappers, quartered

1. In a 4- or 5-quart saucepan, bring 10–12 cups of water to a low boil.
2. While the water is heating, prepare the dim sum filling by combining the seitan and seasonings in a medium bowl. Set aside.
3. Fill a small bowl with water and keep it on hand when assembling the wontons.
4. Place a wonton wrapper on a clean work surface. Dip your fingers into the bowl of water, then moisten the edge of the wrapper with a few drops. Place 1 tablespoon of filling in the center of the wrapper and bring up two opposite corners to enclose the filling, forming a triangle. Press the edges to seal securely, eliminating any air pockets.
5. Bring the right and left corners of this triangle toward the center of the wonton. Press the corners together firmly to seal. Set the filled wonton on a plate and repeat with the remaining filling and wrappers.
6. When the water comes to a rolling boil, carefully add the wontons. Reduce the heat to keep water below a rolling boil. Occasionally stir the wontons with a wooden spoon or paddle to keep them from sticking to the pot or to each other. When cooked, they will float to the top.
7. Remove the wontons with a slotted spoon and place on a plate to cool. Serve them hot or at room temperature, with or without a dipping sauce. The wontons can be refrigerated, then carefully reheated by steaming.

WONTON CROWNS

CALLS FOR:
Ground seitan

SUGGESTED
COOKING METHOD:
Deep-frying

YIELD:
16 crowns

This crispy, deep-fried version of filled wontons will disappear quickly, so be sure to make plenty for everyone! Serve them plain or with your favorite sauce or dip.

1 cup ground seitan (½–¾ pound)
1 recipe seasoning blend of choice (page 21)
16 square wonton wrappers,
or 4 egg roll wrappers, quartered
Oil for deep-frying

1. Heat 2–3 inches of oil in a 3- or 4-quart saucepan.
2. While the oil is heating, prepare the wonton filling by combining the seitan and seasonings in a medium bowl. Set aside.
3. Fill a small bowl with water and keep it on hand when assembling the wontons.
4. Place a wonton wrapper on a clean work surface. Dip your fingers into the bowl of water, then moisten the edge of the wrapper with a few drops. Place 1 tablespoon of filling in the center of the wrapper and bring up two opposite corners to enclose the filling, forming a triangle. Press the edges to seal, eliminating any air pockets.
5. Bring the right and left corners of the triangle together over the center of the wonton. Press the corners together firmly, forming a "crown." Set the crown on a plate and repeat with the remaining filling and wrappers.
6. Without overcrowding the pot, add the wontons in small batches and deep-fry them until golden and crispy (5–8 minutes). Place on absorbent paper towels to remove any excess oil.
7. Serve hot.

EGGLESS SOURDOUGH CRÊPES WITH SPICY SEITAN FILLING

CALLS FOR:
Ground seitan

SUGGESTED
COOKING METHOD:
Pan-simmering

YIELD:
8–10 crêpes

Use the reserved starch water from making homemade seitan as the base for these sourdough crêpes. Keep in mind that the starter needs at least twenty-four hours to ferment. Of course, your favorite crêpe batter can be substituted for the one given below.

SOURDOUGH STARTER
2 cups starch water (from making homemade seitan)
1 cup white corn meal

CRÊPE BATTER
1 cup sourdough starter
1 cup unbleached white flour
1 cup water
¼–½ teaspoon sea salt
1 tablespoon unrefined corn oil

FILLING
2 cups ground seitan (about 1 pound)
2 tablespoons olive oil
1 small onion, sliced thin
2 cups grated carrots
6-ounce can tomato paste
1 cup water
2 tablespoons natural soy sauce
½ teaspoon cayenne pepper

1. To make the starter, combine the starch water and corn-meal in a medium bowl. Cover the bowl with a cloth and leave it undisturbed in a warm place for 24 hours. When the surface appears bubbly, the starter is ready to use. (Stir before using.)
2. To make the crêpe batter, combine 1 cup of starter, the flour, water, salt, and oil in a medium bowl. Mix the ingredients well.
3. Lightly brush an 8- or 9-inch crêpe pan or frying pan with oil and heat it over medium heat. Pour about ¼ cup of

batter in the pan and swirl it around to coat the inside. Turn the crêpe over when its surface is dry and the edges begin to curl. Cook for 2–3 minutes, then remove the crêpe to a plate and let it cool. Repeat with the remaining batter.

4. To make the filling, heat the olive oil in a heavy skillet over medium-high heat. Add the seitan and sauté until browned on all sides (10–15 minutes). Add the onions to the skillet and sauté them, stirring occasionally, until translucent. Add the carrots, tomato paste, water, soy sauce, and cayenne pepper. Mix the ingredients together well, cover the skillet, and simmer about 15 minutes, or until the carrots are tender.

5. Roll up the hot filling in the crêpes.

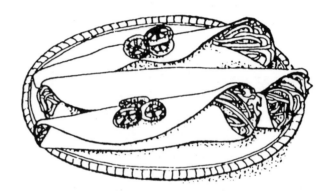

4

SAUCES AND MARINADES

Our apothecary's shop is our garden full of potherbs,
and our doctor is a clove of garlic.

—Anonymous
A Deep Snow (1615)

Probably the best single way to add variety to simple simmered seitan is by flavoring it with a sauce or marinade. Tasty, delicious sauces and gravies are easy to make and have a long shelf life when tightly covered and refrigerated.

In addition to complementing seitan dishes, the sauces and marinades presented in this chapter add mouth-watering dimensions to tofu, vegetable, and fish dishes, as well.

SPICY
BARBECUE MARINADE

YIELD:
About 2¼ cups

This highly spiced sauce is best for marinating seitan cutlets or cubes before broiling them.

2 cups water
2-inch piece kombu
1 recipe Spicy Seasoning Blend (page 21)
2 tablespoons barley malt syrup
2 tablespoons sesame, safflower, or olive oil
1 tablespoon natural soy sauce

1. Combine all the ingredients in a small saucepan and bring to a boil. Reduce the heat to low and simmer 10 minutes.
2. Use hot or cold as a marinade.
3. Covered tightly and refrigerated, Spicy Barbecue Sauce will last for up to two weeks.

MILD
BARBECUE SAUCE

YIELD:
About 1¼ cups

A basic tomato-based, sweet-and-sour barbecue sauce.

1 cup seitan cooking broth, or other seasoned stock
3 tablespoons tomato paste
2 tablespoons brown rice vinegar or cider vinegar
2 teaspoons barley malt syrup

1. Combine all the ingredients in a small saucepan and simmer over low heat for 15 minutes.
2. Use Mild Barbecue Sauce immediately or cover it tightly and refrigerate for up to two weeks.

HICKORY-FLAVORED BARBECUE SAUCE

YIELD:
About 1½ cups

Hearty hickory flavor enhances the rich miso-tomato base of this sauce. Use it as a spread to flavor sandwiches or as an addition to salad dressings, sauces, or marinades.

¼ cup tomato paste
2½ tablespoons cider vinegar
2 tablespoons liquid hickory-smoke flavoring
2 tablespoons barley malt syrup
1½ tablespoons brown rice miso or barley miso
1 tablespoon olive oil
½ medium onion, minced
2 cloves garlic, crushed and minced

1. Combine all the ingredients in a small saucepan and simmer over low heat for 5–10 minutes.
2. Use immediately or cover tightly and refrigerate up to two weeks.

ONION BARBECUE SAUCE

YIELD:
About 1 cup

The addition of onion and allspice to this uncooked sauce makes it a uniquely aromatic and flavorful condiment.

¼ cup barley miso or brown rice miso
¼ cup tomato paste
¼ cup grated onion (about ½ medium onion)
2 cloves garlic, crushed and minced
2 tablespoons olive oil
¼ cup cider vinegar
¼ cup barley malt syrup
¼ teaspoon dry mustard
¼ teaspoon allspice

1. In a small bowl, combine the miso, tomato paste, and onion, and mix thoroughly. Blend in the garlic, oil, and vinegar. Add the barley malt syrup and vigorously mix the ingredients together. Stir in the mustard and allspice.
2. Before using, cover the sauce and let it sit at room temperature for at least 30 minutes to allow the flavors to blend.
3. Cover tightly and refrigerate for up to one week.

QUICK
OIL-FREE GRAVY

YIELD:
About 1¾ cups

This delicious, oil-free gravy is unbelievably easy to make. Using seasoned seitan cooking broth results in a richly flavored sauce that is both fat and cholesterol free!

1 tablespoon kuzu or arrowroot*
½ cup water
1 tablespoon whole wheat pastry flour
¼ cup seitan cooking broth, or other seasoned stock
½ cup plain soymilk or Rice Dream beverage
1 teaspoon natural soy sauce

1. Dissolve the kuzu or arrowroot in half of the water. Add the pastry flour and mix until smooth.
2. In a small saucepan, combine the rest of the water with the remaining ingredients and bring to a boil. Reduce the heat to low and add the kuzu mixture. Continually stir the gravy over low heat until it is thick and creamy (5–8 minutes).
3. Use immediately.

* Can use 2–3 tablespoons of reserved starch water (from making homemade gluten) in place of the arrowroot or kuzu. In this case, reduce the water amount to ¼ cup.

APRICOT BUTTER

YIELD:
1¾–2 cups

Apricot Butter is a delicious chutney-like accompaniment to simmered, oven-braised, or pan-fried seitan.

Coarsely grated rind from 1 medium orange
Coarsely grated rind from 1 medium lemon
¼ teaspoon cinnamon
Pinch sea salt
3 cups water
1 cup unsulphured dried apricots
3 tablespoons rice syrup

1. In a small saucepan, combine the orange rind, lemon rind, cinnamon, salt, and water. Add the apricots and simmer over low heat, covered, until they are tender (about 30 minutes).
2. Transfer the cooked apricots to a blender or food mill and purée them. Return the purée to the pan, add the rice syrup, and simmer for 5–10 minutes. Chill before serving.
3. Covered and refrigerated, Apricot Butter will last for up to two weeks.

TERIYAKI MARINADE

YIELD:
About 1 cup

Mirin, a Japanese cooking wine, adds a unique flavor to this marinade.

½ cup natural soy sauce
3 tablespoons mirin
2 tablespoons brown rice syrup
1 tablespoon brown rice vinegar or cider vinegar
1 tablespoon paprika
A few drops Chinese hot pepper oil

1. Combine all the ingredients in a small bowl.
2. Use immediately or refrigerate, tightly covered, for up to two weeks. Shake or stir well before using.

THICK MISO MARINADE

YIELD:
About 1½ cups

This marinade is perfect for seasoning seitan, vegetables, or tofu dishes.

2 tablespoons barley miso or brown rice miso
½ cup water
2 tablespoons brown rice vinegar
1 tablespoon toasted (dark) sesame oil
1 tablespoon mirin
1 tablespoon barley malt syrup

1. In a small bowl, mix the miso and water together to form a smooth paste. Add the remaining ingredients one at a time, mixing well after each addition.
2. Use immediately or refrigerate, tightly covered, for up to two weeks. Shake or stir well before using.

TANGY MUSTARD SAUCE

YIELD:
About ¾ cup

Tangy Mustard Sauce complements many seitan dishes. It is the perfect accompaniment for Quick and Tangy Seitan Cubes (page 35) and Green and Golden Spirals (page 40).

½ cup Dijon-style mustard
2 tablespoons rice syrup
1 teaspoon natural soy sauce
1 tablespoon arrowroot or kuzu
¾ cup water

1. In a small pan, combine the mustard, rice syrup, and soy sauce.
2. In a small bowl, dissolve the arrowroot in the water, then add it to the pan. Stir until smooth.
3. Heat the ingredients over low heat, stirring until the sauce thickens (about 5 minutes). Use hot or cold.
4. Cover tightly and refrigerate for up to one week. (If you can keep it around that long!)

BASIC MARINARA SAUCE

YIELD:
4 quarts

Made in a four-quart batch, this sauce is perfect for freezing in meal-size portions.

4 cups diced onions (about 5–6 medium onions)
6 cloves garlic, crushed and chopped
½ cup olive oil
4 cups diced celery
2 teaspoons sea salt
2 cups water
2 tablespoons oregano
2 tablespoons basil
¼ teaspoon allspice
1 can (6 ounces) tomato paste
2 cans (35 ounces each) whole peeled tomatoes, including juice
2 cans (28 ounces each) crushed peeled tomatoes
2 teaspoons barley malt syrup
¼ cup brown rice miso

1. In a 5- to 8-quart stockpot, sauté the onions and garlic in the oil until they are lightly browned. Add the celery, salt, and water, and simmer 5 minutes.
2. To the pot, add the oregano, basil, allspice, tomato paste, whole tomatoes, crushed tomatoes, and barley malt syrup. Stir to combine the ingredients well.
3. Remove about ½ cup of sauce from the pot and place it in a small bowl with the miso. Combine well to form a smooth paste, then return the diluted miso to the pot.
4. Simmer the sauce over low heat, loosely covered, for 1 hour. Remove the cover and simmer another 2 hours while stirring occasionally.
5. Use the sauce immediately or save it for a later use. It stores well in the refrigerator, and freezes beautifully.

YIELD:

About 1½ cups

MEDITERRANEAN MARINADE

Tarragon and capers add to the Mediterranean flavor of this marinade.

½ cup lemon juice
¼ cup olive oil
2 tablespoons natural soy sauce
1 tablespoon tarragon
½ teaspoon oregano
½ teaspoon sea salt
Coarsely grated rind from ½ medium lemon
1 tablespoon capers, rinsed and drained

1. Combine all the ingredients except the capers in a small saucepan and heat to just below the boiling point.
2. Immediately pour this hot liquid over the seitan (or other food) you wish to marinate. Top with the capers and toss the ingredients together to evenly coat.
3. Place the dish in the refrigerator and marinate. Remove 30 minutes before serving. Serve at room temperature for the fullest flavor.

YIELD:

About 1 cup

SALSA PICANTE

This flavorful uncooked sauce is quick and easy to make. Its lively blend of ingredients is a welcome addition to dishes that are complemented by a tomato-based sweet-and-sour flavor. Try it with Corn Doggies (page 41).

¼ cup brown rice miso or barley miso
¼ cup tomato paste
¼ cup grated onion (about ½ medium onion)
1 teaspoon finely minced garlic
2 tablespoons olive oil
¼ cup cider vinegar
¼ cup barley malt syrup
¼ teaspoon dry mustard
¼ teaspoon allspice

1. In a small bowl, combine the miso, tomato paste, and onion. Mix well. Add the garlic, oil, vinegar, and barley malt syrup, mixing the ingredients vigorously. Blend in the mustard and allspice.
2. Allow the salsa to sit at room temperature for at least 30 minutes to allow the flavors to blend.
3. Cover tightly and refrigerate up to ten days.

CHICKPEA GRAVY

YIELD:
About 1½ cups

Be sure to try Mini-Croquettes (page 42) smothered in this savory golden-colored gravy.

2 tablespoons corn oil
¼ cup chickpea flour
¾ cup plain soymilk or Rice Dream beverage
½ cup water
¼ cup grated onion (about ½ medium onion)
¼ teaspoon allspice
¼ teaspoon black pepper
2 tablespoons natural soy sauce
2 tablespoons cider vinegar

1. In a small saucepan, heat the oil over low heat.
2. Remove the pan from the heat. Sprinkle the chickpea flour over the oil, and blend well with a fork or whisk. Return the pan to the heat and continue stirring the mixture for 2–3 minutes.
3. Slowly add the soymilk and water to the pan, while stirring constantly. Add the remaining ingredients and continue to stir the gravy as it simmers and thickens (about 20 minutes). Use hot.
4. Covered tightly and refrigerated, this gravy will keep for two days. Reheat over a medium heat.

RED CHILIES MARENGO

YIELD:
About 1½ cups

The ultimate companion to Seitan Bandito (page 46), this condiment is a flavorful addition to stews, soups, and casseroles. It is also a delicious marinade for tofu, seitan, and fish, as well as a lively dip for chips and raw vegetables.

3 ounces dried Ancho chilies, halved and seeded
3 cups boiling water
8 cloves garlic
¼ teaspoon cumin
¼ teaspoon oregano
¼–½ cup brown rice miso or barley miso

1. In a small heat-proof bowl, cover the chilies with the boiling water. Let them soak about 30 minutes. (The soaking water will turn red.)
2. Transfer the chilies to a blender or food processor along with the garlic and a little of the soaking water. Purée the ingredients, adding more soaking water as needed to form a paste.
3. Add the cumin, oregano, and miso, and blend well.
4. Transfer the mixture to a small saucepan and simmer over low heat for 10 minutes. Serve warm, at room temperature, or chilled.
5. Tightly covered and refrigerated, this salsa will keep up to two weeks.

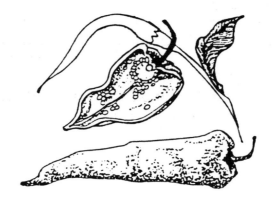

5

SOUPS AND
STEWS

To make a good soup, the pot must only simmer or "smile."
—French Proverb

A satisfying and delicious soup or stew can serve as
the perfect prelude to a meal or a meal in itself.
This chapter shows how to create nourishing soups and
stews using seitan as a principle ingredient and as a
secondary ingredient. Whether it is used as dumplings,
croutons, or a main ingredient, seitan will enhance
your favorite soups and provide an opportunity for
you to experiment with some new dishes. Hot and
Sour Cabbage Soup (page 69), Savory Dumplings in
Vegetable-Lemon Soup (page 67), and Seitan Stew
Provençal (page 73) are just a few of the dishes in this
chapter. I hope you will be inspired to add seitan to
familiar soups and stews, as well as explore some new
and unusual dishes that you have never tried before.

GOLDEN SQUASH POTAGE

CALLS FOR:
Seitan slices,
or seitan sausage

SUGGESTED
COOKING METHODS:
Pan-frying,
then simmering

YIELD:
Serves 6

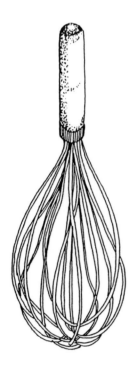

Creamy and elegant, this easy-to-prepare soup is a feast for the eyes. The naturally sweet, rich flavor of butternut squash is well suited to be part of a simple brunch or a festive holiday meal.

1 cup (about ½ pound) seitan slices (¼ inch), or 2 links
Spicy Seitan Sausage (page 126), cut into ¼-inch rounds
1 medium butternut squash
4 cups water
1 teaspoon sea salt
¼ teaspoon allspice
1 cup plain soymilk, or Rice Dream beverage
2–3 tablespoons corn oil or sesame oil
3 tablespoons minced fresh parsley, or 1 tablespoon dried

1. Cut the squash in half, remove the seeds, and peel (if not organic). Cut into 1-inch cubes.
2. In a large pot, bring the water to a medium boil and cook the squash until tender (about 15 minutes).
3. Reserving the cooking water, transfer the squash to a blender or food processor. Adding the reserved cooking water a little at a time, purée the squash to a creamy consistency. Return the squash to the pot and whisk in the salt, allspice, and soymilk. Cover the purée and keep it warm over low heat.
4. In a heavy pan or skillet, cook the seitan slices in the oil until they are well-browned on both sides (about 5 minutes per side). Place on absorbent paper towels to remove any excess oil.
5. About 10 minutes before serving the soup, add the seitan.
6. Ladle the hot soup into individual bowls and garnish with a sprinkle of parsley.

Hearty Garden Soup with Chickpeas and Golden Dumplings

CALLS FOR:
Gluten made from
gluten flour

SUGGESTED
COOKING METHODS:
Deep-frying,
then pan-simmering

YIELD:
6–8 servings

Deep-fried seitan dumplings add succulent rich flavor to this hearty vegetable-filled soup.

1 tablespoon sesame oil
1 medium onion, diced
1 cup diced celery
2 cups diced carrots
8 cups water
4-inch piece kombu, broken into ¼-inch pieces
4 cups cooked chickpeas
1 teaspoon sea salt
1 cup ¼-inch zucchini half-rounds
1 cup green beans (1-inch pieces)
2 tablespoons natural soy sauce
Snipped fresh chives for garnish

DUMPLINGS
⅔ cup gluten flour
½ cup water
2 tablespoons plain soymilk or Rice Dream beverage
Oil for deep-frying

1. In a large pot, heat the sesame oil over low heat. Add the onion and sauté until translucent (about 5 minutes). Add the celery and carrots, and continue to sauté the vegetables for 5 minutes. Add the water, kombu, chickpeas, and salt, and bring the ingredients to a boil. Reduce the heat and simmer about 30 minutes.

2. While the soup is simmering, prepare the dumplings. Place the gluten flour in a medium bowl, add the water and soymilk, and mix the ingredients vigorously with a fork to create a fairly soft dough. Let the dough rest for 10–15 minutes.

3. While the dough is resting, heat 2–3 inches of oil in a 3- or 4-quart saucepan. When the oil is hot, carefully drop the gluten dough by the tablespoon into the oil. Deep-fry the dumplings until they are golden (5–8 minutes). Place on absorbent paper towels to remove any excess oil.

4. Add the dumplings to the soup, gently pressing them against the sides of the pot to flatten them a bit.

5. Finally, add the zucchini and green beans to the soup, and simmer them until tender but not overcooked (about 10 minutes).

6. Just before serving the soup, add the soy sauce. Ladle the hot soup into individual serving bowls, and garnish each serving with a sprinkling of fresh chives.

SAVORY DUMPLINGS IN VEGETABLE-LEMON SOUP

CALLS FOR:
Gluten made from
gluten flour

SUGGESTED
COOKING METHOD:
Pan-simmering

YIELD:
6 servings

Combining seasonings and soymilk with gluten flour produces tender dumplings that are perfect in this light vegetable soup. Each serving is garnished with a wedge of fresh lemon and a sprig of watercress, creating a visually appealing presentation.

8 cups water
3-inch piece kombu
1 cup onion slices
1 carrot, sliced into ⅛-inch rounds
½ head cauliflower, cut into 1-inch flowerets
1 teaspoon sea salt
1 tablespoon natural soy sauce
1 lemon, cut crosswise into ⅛-inch slices
Watercress springs or fresh dill for garnish

DUMPLINGS
¾ cup gluten flour
1 recipe Savory Seasoning Blend (page 21)
1 cup plain soymilk, or Rice Dream beverage
1 teaspoon sesame oil

1. In a 4-quart saucepan, heat the water over medium heat. When the water heats to just below the boiling point, add the kombu and simmer for 5 minutes. Remove the kombu, cut it into thin strips, and return it to the soup. Add the onion, carrot, cauliflower, salt, and soy sauce. Let the soup simmer.
2. Prepare the dumplings as the soup simmers. In a medium bowl, combine the flour and Savory Seasoning Blend. Add the soymilk and oil, mixing it vigorously with a fork. Mix well and knead the dough until it has a uniform consistency. Let the dough rest for 5 minutes.
3. Break off 1-inch pieces of the gluten and lower them one by one into the hot soup. Stir the dumplings to prevent them from sticking together. Simmer for 15–20 minutes.
4. Place one lemon slice in the bottom of each individual serving bowl. Ladle the hot soup into the bowl, and garnish the soup with watercress or dill.

BLACK BEAN SOUP

CALLS FOR:
Seitan cubes

SUGGESTED
COOKING METHODS:
Pan-frying,
then simmering

YIELD:
6 servings

This garlic-laden, richly flavored soup has undertones of cumin and cayenne pepper. The hour-and-a-half cooking time ensures well-blended flavors. When accompanied by a crisp green salad and hot cornbread, this soup is a complete meal.

2–4 cups (1–2 pounds) seitan cubes (1-inch)
6 tablespoons olive oil or sesame oil
1 medium onion, diced
8 cloves garlic, crushed and minced
4 cups cooked black beans
10 cups water
2 teaspoons sea salt
1 tablespoon cumin
2 teaspoons oregano
1 bay leaf
¼ teaspoon cayenne pepper
1 tablespoon natural soy sauce
1 sweet red pepper, diced
2 tablespoons mirin
2 tablespoons lemon juice
1 tablespoon barley malt syrup
¼ cup finely chopped fresh parsley

1. In a large, heavy stockpot, heat 3 tablespoons of the oil over low heat. Add the onion and garlic, and sauté until the onion is translucent (about 5 minutes). Add the beans, water, salt, cumin, oregano, bay leaf, and cayenne pepper. Simmer the soup, uncovered, for about 1 hour, stirring occasionally.
2. Heat the remaining oil in a skillet, and pan-fry the seitan cubes over medium heat for about 10 minutes. Sprinkle with soy sauce and continue to cook the cubes until well browned and somewhat crispy on all sides.
3. After the soup has simmered for about 1 hour, add the seitan cubes along with their cooking liquid to the soup. Add the red pepper, mirin, lemon juice, barley malt syrup, and parsley. Simmer another 15–30 minutes.
4. Black Bean Soup is best when served hot.

HOT AND SOUR CABBAGE SOUP

CALLS FOR:
Gluten

SUGGESTED
COOKING METHODS:
Pan-frying,
then simmering

YIELD:
6 servings

This variation of the traditional Chinese soup is simple to prepare. Its hearty smoky flavor comes from chewy pan-fried strips of gluten.

½ cup thin gluten strips
½ medium-size green or white cabbage
2 tablespoons sesame oil
1 medium onion, sliced thin
1½ teaspoons sea salt
8 cups water or stock
1 pound firm tofu, cut into ½-inch cubes
¼ teaspoon black pepper
¼ teaspoon Chinese hot pepper oil
¼ cup natural soy sauce
¼ cup lemon juice
2 tablespoons arrowroot or kuzu
Slivered scallion greens for garnish

1. Remove and discard the cabbage core. Cut the cabbage lengthwise into thirds, then finely shred the cabbage crosswise. Set aside.
2. In a large pot, heat the sesame oil over medium heat. Add the gluten strips and fry them until browned (about 5 minutes), stirring to prevent them from sticking. Add the onion, salt, and cabbage. Continue to sauté the vegetables until they are translucent.
3. Add enough hot water or stock to almost cover the vegetables and bring to a boil. Add the tofu, black pepper, and hot pepper oil. Simmer for 20 minutes.
4. Combine the soy sauce and lemon juice, then add to the arrowroot and mix until dissolved. Add this mixture to the hot soup. Stir the soup to avoid creating lumps. (The soup will thicken slightly.) Be careful not to overheat the soup, or its glaze-like quality will be lost.
5. Serve the soup immediately, garnished with scallions.

COUNTRY VEGETABLE SOUP

CALLS FOR:
Seitan cubes

SUGGESTED
COOKING METHOD:
Pan-frying

YIELD:
6 servings

This is one of those old-fashioned soups that gets better the longer it simmers. The crispy seasoned seitan cubes are added to the soup just before serving.

2 cups (about 1 pound) seitan cubes (½ inch)
3 tablespoons olive oil
1 large onion, quartered, then cut crosswise
into ½-inch slices
2 stalks celery, cut into ½-inch pieces
2 large potatoes, cut into 1-inch cubes
4 cups thinly sliced cabbage
4 cups water
1 can (35 ounces) crushed tomatoes
1 cup finely chopped fresh fennel
1 teaspoon sea salt
2 bay leaves
2 cloves garlic, crushed and minced
¼ teaspoon allspice
¾ teaspoon black pepper
¾ teaspoon sage

1. In a large stockpot, heat 1 tablespoon of the oil over medium heat. Add the onions, celery, cabbage, and potatoes. Sauté the vegetables about 5 minutes, then add the water, tomatoes, fennel, salt, bay leaves, garlic, and allspice. Bring the ingredients to a light boil, reduce the heat, and simmer the soup until the vegetables are tender (about 20 minutes.) For best results allow the soup to simmer about 1 hour.
2. While the soup simmers, heat the remaining 2 tablespoons of oil in a skillet over medium heat. Add the black pepper and sage, and sauté for about 30 seconds. Add the seitan cubes and heat them until well-browned and crispy on all sides (8–15 minutes). Remove the cooked cubes to a bowl, cover, and set aside.
3. To serve, place 6 or 7 seitan cubes in each individual bowl, then top with the hot soup.

QUICK STEW

CALLS FOR:
Gluten

SUGGESTED
COOKING METHOD:
Pressure-cooking

YIELD:
8 servings

This delicious, hearty dish is the perfect fare when time is at a premium. Feel free to change or add any vegetables to the ones suggested below.

4 cups gluten (about 3 pounds),
formed into bite-size pieces or balls
1 double recipe Basic Broth (page 20)
2 large onions, quartered
3 medium carrots, cut into 1-inch rounds
2 stalks celery, cut into 1-inch slices
¼ cup wheat starch
3 tablespoons mirin
3 cloves garlic, minced
¼ cup natural soy sauce, or to taste
Slivered scallions for garnish

1. In a pressure cooker, bring the Basic Broth to a low boil. Slowly add the gluten pieces to the broth.
2. Cover and seal the pressure cooker and raise the heat. When the cooker comes to pressure, reduce the heat and simmer the gluten about 20 minutes.
3. Reduce the pressure by placing the pot in the sink and running cool water over the top. When all the pressure has been released, remove the cover and add the vegetables. Simmer the vegetables until they are tender, or cover the cooker and increase the pressure for 2 minutes.
4. While the vegetables are cooking, combine the wheat starch, mirin, garlic, and soy sauce in a small bowl and set aside.
5. When the vegetables are tender, slowly add the wheat-starch mixture to the pot and stir over low heat until the stew is thick. (Adjust the thickness with more starch or water as needed.)
6. Garnish individual servings with scallions.

Oven-Braised Sweet-and-Spicy Stew with Dried Fruit

CALLS FOR:
Seitan cubes

SUGGESTED
COOKING METHODS:
Sautéing,
then oven-braising

YIELD:
6 servings

Overtones of bay leaf and cumin accent the subtle natural sweetness of dried fruit in this hearty stew. This dish, which takes less than an hour to cook, is a delicious addition to a winter holiday buffet.

3 cups (about 1½ pound) seitan cubes (1 inch)
¼ cup raisins
⅔ cup dried apples
⅔ cup dried apricots
1 cup water
1 cup dry red wine
½ cup cider vinegar
2 shallots, minced
½ teaspoon cumin
1 large bay leaf
3 tablespoons olive oil
3 large carrots, cut into ¾-inch chunks

1. Preheat the oven to 400°F.
2. In a 2-quart saucepan, combine the raisins, apples, apricots, water, wine, vinegar, shallots, cumin, and bay leaf. Over high heat, bring the ingredients to a low boil, then remove the pan from the heat and let the mixture stand, allowing the dried fruit to soften.
3. Heat the oil in a Dutch oven or flameproof casserole over medium heat. Add the seitan cubes and sauté them until they are well browned and crispy on all sides (about 15 minutes).
4. Reserving the juice, drain the softened dried fruit and add it to the seitan along with the carrots. Simmer the seitan and fruit together for 5 minutes. Add the reserved seasoned juice, and cover tightly.
5. Reduce the oven temperature to 350°F. Cook the stew in the oven until the carrots are tender (about 1 hour).
6. Remove the stew from the oven and stir once before serving.

SEITAN STEW PROVENÇAL

CALLS FOR:
Seitan cubes

SUGGESTED
COOKING METHODS:
Pan-frying,
then simmering

YIELD:
6 servings

In less than forty-five minutes you can turn simple, healthful ingredients into a special-occasion meal. Crusty whole wheat French bread and a fragrant salad round out this sumptuous aromatic stew.

4 cups (about 2 pounds) seitan cubes (1 inch)
⅓ cup olive oil
4 cloves garlic, crushed and minced
1 large onion, diced
3 celery stalks, cut into 1-inch pieces
2 carrots, cut into ¼-inch rounds
1 medium turnip or 3-inch piece daikon radish,
cut into ½-inch cubes
4 cups water
8 small plum tomatoes, quartered
1 cup cooked white beans
1 cup pitted black olives
¾ cup dry red wine
2 bay leaves
1 cup thick starch water*
¼ cup natural soy sauce
¼ cup minced fresh parsley

COATING MIX
½ cup whole wheat pastry flour
3 tablespoons parsley flakes
3 tablespoons paprika
1 tablespoon thyme
2 teaspoons basil
1 teaspoon sea salt
1 teaspoon celery seeds
1 teaspoon garlic granules
½ teaspoon black pepper
½ teaspoon allspice

* Use reserved starch water from preparing homemade gluten, or dissolve
2 tablespoons arrowroot or kuzu in 1 cup water.

1. Prepare the seasoned coating mixture by combining all the coating-mix ingredients in a medium bowl.

2. Roll the seitan in the coating mix, pressing the mixture into the cubes. Set the coated cubes aside.
3. In a large pot, heat the olive oil over medium heat. Add the seitan cubes and brown them well on all sides (about 15 minutes).
4. To the browned cubes, add the garlic, onion, celery, carrots, turnip, and water. Cover the pot and allow the stew to reach a low boil.
5. When the ingredients come to a boil, reduce the heat to low and add the tomatoes, beans, olives, wine, and bay leaves. Simmer until the carrots are tender (about 20 minutes).
6. Combine the soy sauce with the starch water, then slowly add it to the stew, stirring to keep the sauce smooth. Continue to simmer the stew, stirring as it thickens (about 5–8 minutes). Add more water as needed.
7. Just before serving, add the fresh parsley.

SEITAN WITH ONIONS AND CARROTS BAKED IN HEAVENLY CREAMY DILL SAUCE

CALLS FOR:
Seitan cubes

SUGGESTED COOKING METHOD:
Baking

YIELD:
6–8 servings

A little mirin and dill season the creamy sauce in this simple baked stew of seitan cubes, onions, and carrots. Easy to assemble, this dish takes only forty-five minutes to bake. Hearty enough to enjoy on its own, this stew can also be served with the grain of your choice.

3 teaspoons sesame oil
2 medium onions, diced
2 large carrots, sliced into ½-inch rounds
4 cups (about 2 pounds) seitan cubes (1 inch)
2 tablespoons whole wheat pastry flour
¼ teaspoon sea salt
1 cup water
¾ cup plain soymilk or Rice Dream beverage
1 tablespoon finely chopped fresh dill
¼ teaspoon black pepper

DILL SAUCE
½ cup plain soymilk or Rice Dream beverage
2 tablespoons chickpea flour
1 tablespoon mirin
1 tablespoon finely chopped fresh dill
¼ teaspoon sea salt

1. Preheat the oven to 350°F.
2. Heat the oil in a flameproof casserole over medium heat. Add the onion, carrots, and seitan, and sauté for 3–5 minutes.
3. Sprinkle the pastry flour and sea salt over the seitan and vegetables. Continue to sauté the ingredients for a few minutes, stirring frequently. Add the water, soymilk, dill, and pepper to the casserole. Stir the ingredients occasionally for about 5 minutes until the liquid begins to thicken.
4. Cover the casserole, transfer it to the oven, and bake until the carrots are tender (45–60 minutes).

5. Remove the stew from the oven and place it on the stove-top over very low heat.

6. Prepare the dill sauce. First, make a loose smooth paste by adding the soymilk to the chickpea flour. Add the mirin, dill, and sea salt. Slowly add this mixture to the stew, stirring constantly until the sauce thickens. Continue to simmer the stew for about 15 minutes.

7. Serve the hot stew either alone or with brown rice, couscous, millet, or broad noodles.

HOMESTYLE STEW

CALLS FOR:
Seitan cutlets

SUGGESTED
COOKING METHODS:
Deep-frying,
then pan-simmering

YIELD:
6 servings

Experiment with your choice of herbs and spices in the seitan batter. The flavors will transfer to the stew.

6 seitan cutlets (about 1½ pounds), quartered
3 medium carrots, cut into ¼-inch rounds
5 stalks celery, cut into 1-inch pieces
2 cups seasoned stock
Oil for deep-frying
3 tablespoons arrowroot*
¾ cup plain soymilk or Rice Dream beverage
¼ cup natural soy sauce, or to taste

BATTER
1 cup whole wheat pastry flour
½ cup corn flour
1 tablespoon arrowroot
1 tablespoon dried parsley
1 tablespoon dried fenugreek
1 teaspoon dried dill
1 teaspoon ground black pepper
¾ teaspoon sea salt
½ teaspoon paprika
1¼ cups water

* Can use ¼–½ cup thick starch water (from making homemade gluten) in place of the arrowroot.

1. Combine all the batter ingredients in a medium bowl and mix together well. Refrigerate the batter for at least 10 minutes.
2. Place the celery on top of the carrots in a large heavy pot with a tight-fitting lid. Add the broth and bring to a low boil. Reduce the heat and simmer until the carrots are tender (10–15 minutes).
3. While the broth is simmering, heat 2–3 inches of oil in a 3- or 4-quart saucepan. While the oil is heating, coat the seitan pieces in the batter. Without overcrowding the pot, add the seitan in small batches and deep-fry until golden brown (about 5 minutes). Place on absorbent paper towels to remove any excess oil.
4. Place the arrowroot in a small bowl. Slowly add the soymilk, stirring constantly until a smooth, well-blended mixture is formed. Add this mixture to the simmering vegetables and stir the ingredients until the broth becomes thick and glossy. Add the soy sauce.
5. Carefully add the seitan and scallions to the pot. Cover and simmer the stew until the seitan is thoroughly heated (5–8 minutes).
6. Serve the hot stew over your favorite whole grain or pasta.

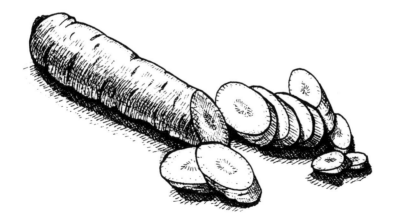

STEW IN GOLDEN SAUCE

CALLS FOR:
Gluten

SUGGESTED
COOKING METHOD:
Pan-simmering

YIELD:
6–8 servings

Unevenly shaped seitan pieces and bright bits of vegetables add visual interest to this golden stew. Serve it over broad egg noodles or fettuccine.

FOR COOKING GLUTEN
2 cups gluten
2-inch piece kombu
6 cups water
¼ cup natural soy sauce
1 tablespoon olive oil or sesame oil
2 tablespoons nutritional yeast
½ teaspoon turmeric

STEW INGREDIENTS
15–20 small white onions
1 large carrot, cut into ¼-inch rounds
2 celery stalks, cut into ½-inch pieces
Water to cover vegetables
1 teaspoon sea salt
1 cup chickpea flour
¼ cup thick starch water*
2 cups frozen or freshly shelled green peas

* Can use reserved starch water from making homemade gluten, or 1½ teaspoons arrowroot or kuzu dissolved in ¼ cup water.

1. To cook the gluten, first bring the kombu and water to boil in a large pot. Reduce the heat to medium and add the soy sauce, oil, yeast, and turmeric.
2. Divide the gluten into 2 pieces, and carefully lower 1 of the pieces into the water. Using 2 forks, gently pull apart the large piece of gluten as it cooks, holding the forks in one position for about 20 seconds. Reposition the forks and repeat the pulling and holding until the gluten has been pulled apart into bite-size pieces. Repeat with the remaining piece of gluten.
3. Reduce the heat to low and simmer gently, uncovered, for 30 minutes, until the seitan absorbs the stock.

4. While the seitan is simmering, prepare the stew. Place the onions, carrots, and celery in another large pot. Add enough water to cover all but 1 inch of the vegetables. Bring the ingredients to a boil, then reduce the heat to low. Add the salt. Simmer until the carrots and onions are tender (about 15 minutes).

5. Remove some of the stew broth and combine it with the chickpea flour to form a paste. Add this paste to the stew, continuing to stir as the broth thickens. If the broth is too thin, add the starch water and continue to stir until the desired consistency is reached.

6. Ten minutes before serving the stew, add the peas and seitan. Serve plain or over noodles.

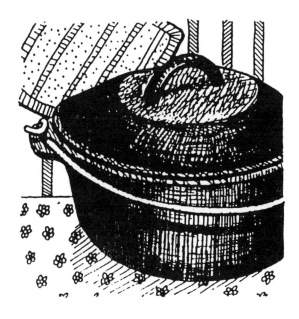

6

SALADS AND SALAD DRESSINGS

Oh, herbaceous treat!
Back to the world he'd turn his fleeting soul,
And plunge his fingers in the salad bowl;
Serenely full the epicure would say,
"Fate cannot harm me, I have dined today."

—Sydney Smith (1771–1845)
A Receipt for a Salad

When used in salads, seitan can appear in a variety of forms. For instance, flavorful seitan dumplings are called for in Escarole and Seitan Salad with Anchovy-Tarragon Vinaigrette (page 97); spicy braised strips are used in Hot Wilted Spinach Salad with Sesame-Chili Braised Seitan (page 101); and deep-fried gluten is found in the Fragrant Chinese Pasta Salad (page 91). Crispy seitan "croutons" can add a tasty accent to simple, lightly dressed greens, while savory strips can be a tasty addition to whole-meal salads.

As most of the recipes in this chapter call for seasoned, ready-to-eat seitan, preparing the salads is quick and easy. We're sure you will enjoy seitan in salads as much as you enjoy it in other dishes.

GREEN BEAN AND TOASTED WALNUT SALAD WITH CREAMY UMEBOSHI DRESSING

CALLS FOR:
Seitan strips

SUGGESTED
COOKING METHOD:
None

YIELD:
6 servings

Toasted walnuts add a flavorful crunch to this easy-to-prepare salad.

1½ cups (about ¾ pound) seitan strips (1½ x ½ inches)
¾ cup coarsely chopped walnuts
½ red onion, sliced very thin
1½ pounds green beans, trimmed and cut into thirds

CREAMY UMEBOSHI DRESSING
1½ tablespoons umeboshi paste
½ cup plain soymilk or Rice Dream beverage
2 teaspoons sesame oil or safflower oil
½ teaspoon brown rice vinegar
1 teaspoon chopped fresh dill
1 teaspoon chopped fresh thyme

1. In a small bowl, prepare the dressing by adding the soymilk, a little at a time, to the umeboshi paste. Mix well with a fork or whisk. Add the oil, brown rice vinegar, dill, and thyme, and continue to mix. Cover and refrigerate the dressing until ready to use.
2. While stirring them constantly, toast the walnuts in a cast iron frying pan over medium heat for about 5 minutes, or bake them in a 350°F oven for 15 minutes. Allow the walnuts to cool before adding them, along with the onion slices, to the umeboshi dressing.
3. Steam the beans until they are just tender and bright green in color. Drain them in a colander, then plunge them into cold water to stop the cooking and set the bright color. Drain the beans and pat them dry.
4. Place the beans and half the seitan strips in a bowl, add the dressing, and toss lightly. Arrange the salad on a platter and top with the remaining seitan strips.

MEDITERRANEAN VEGETABLE MEDLEY

CALLS FOR:
Gluten

SUGGESTED
COOKING METHOD:
Boiling

YIELD:
6 servings

This refreshing vegetable combination can be mixed with your favorite cooked pasta for a satisfying warm-weather main dish.

2 cups gluten
2 leeks
12 cups water
2 carrots, cut into ¼-inch rounds
3-inch piece kombu
1 recipe Savory Seasoning Blend (page 21), optional
½ red onion, sliced into thin rings
1 sweet red pepper, diced
1 zucchini, cut into thin rounds

MARINADE
½ cup lemon juice
3–4 tablespoons olive oil
2 tablespoons natural soy sauce
3 teaspoons tarragon
1 tablespoon capers
½ teaspoon oregano
Coarsely grated rind from ½ lemon

1. Cut the leeks in half lengthwise, then wash them well under cold running water to remove any dirt or sand. Cut the halves crosswise into ¼-inch pieces.
2. Combine the water, leeks, carrots, kombu, and Savory Seasoning Blend (if using) in a large pot. Bring the ingredients to a boil, then reduce the heat to low.
3. Break off small pieces of gluten and add them one by one to the pot. Simmer the gluten and vegetables, partially covered, for 45–60 minutes.
4. While the gluten is simmering, combine all the marinade ingredients together in a small bowl and set aside.

5. Using a slotted spoon, transfer the cooked gluten (seitan) and vegetables to a large bowl. Reserve the remaining broth for another use.*
6. Add the onion, red pepper, and zucchini to the seitan and vegetables. Cover with the marinade and mix together well.
7. Refrigerate the salad at least 20 minutes before serving.

* This versatile broth is useful in soups, sauces, and gravies. Can also be used as the cooking liquid for grains and pastas.

HEARTY SEITAN SALAD WITH NEW RED POTATOES

CALLS FOR:
Seitan slices

SUGGESTED COOKING METHOD:
Broiling

YIELD:
6 servings

Dijon mustard dressing provides the perfect background for this salad of marinated red potatoes and broiled seitan.

1½ cups (about ¾ pound) seitan slices
(2-inch squares about ⅛ inch thick)
½ teaspoon paprika
6 medium red potatoes, unpeeled and cut into large cubes
¼ cup minced parsley
½ cup grated carrot for garnish
Boston or bibb lettuce to use as a bed for the salad

MARINADE
¼ cup olive oil
3 tablespoons cider vinegar
2½ tablespoons natural soy sauce

DRESSING
Remaining seitan marinade
1 or 2 garlic cloves, crushed and minced
2 scallions, cut very fine
1 tablespoon cider vinegar
½ teaspoon Dijon-style mustard

1. Combine the marinade ingredients in a medium bowl, and marinate the seitan slices for 45–60 minutes. (Turn the slices every 10–15 minutes as they marinate.)
2. Remove the marinated seitan, pressing each piece against the side of the bowl to remove excess marinade. Arrange the pieces on a lightly oiled baking sheet and sprinkle with paprika. Broil the seitan 6 inches from the heat source for 2–3 minutes on each side.
3. Cook the potatoes in gently boiling, lightly salted water until they are tender but not mushy (about 10 minutes).
4. While the potatoes are cooking, combine all the dressing ingredients in a large bowl and mix together well.
5. Drain the cooked potatoes and add them to the dressing while they are still hot. Refrigerate for 15 minutes, then add the seitan and parsley. Toss the salad carefully.
6. Spoon the salad (either chilled or at room temperature) onto a bed of Boston or bibb lettuce. Garnish with grated carrots before serving.

PRESSED WINTER SALAD WITH RADISHES

CALLS FOR:
Seitan strips

SUGGESTED COOKING METHOD:
None

YIELD:
4–6 servings

A "pressed" salad is one in which the vegetables have been compressed under a weight to remove the water. In Japan, napa cabbage is traditionally used. In this version, red radishes, scallions, and seitan strips are also included. Although the pressing can take take up to two hours, the actual preparation-time is quite short.

1 cup (about ½ pound) seitan strips (2 x ¼ inches)
½ medium head Chinese (napa) cabbage,
shredded into 2-inch strips
2 scallions, sliced into 2-inch strips
6 red radishes with leaves, sliced thin
1 tablespoon sea salt
1 tablespoon sesame oil
2 tablespoons freshly squeezed lemon juice
1 tablespoon toasted sesame seeds

1. In a large mixing bowl, combine the cabbage, scallions, radishes, and radish leaves with the sea salt. Mix well by hand, thoroughly but gently rubbing the salt into the vegetables.

2. To press the salad, you can use one of two methods. For one method, you can use a vegetable press.* Place the salted vegetables into the press and tighten the pressure as much as possible. Increase the pressure every 15 minutes (if possible). If you do not have a vegetable press, simply place the salted vegetables in a deep bowl and cover them with a plate. Place a 5 to 10-pound weight (a clean jar filled with water or beans, or a heavy, well-washed rock) on top of the plate. Press the vegetables until most of the water has been extracted (up to 2 hours).

3. Pour off and discard the "juice" from the pressed vegetables. Add the sesame oil and lemon juice to the vegetables and combine well. Garnish with the seitan strips and sesame seeds.

4. Refrigerate the salad for 10 minutes before serving.

5. Covered tightly and refrigerated, this salad will keep for up to two days.

* Vegetable presses are available in most Asian markets.

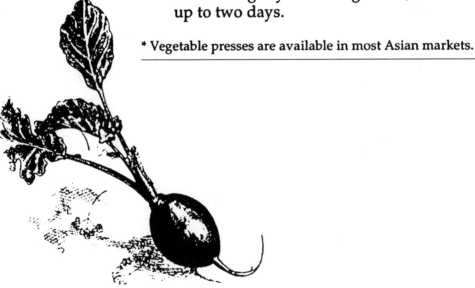

SAVORY SEITAN SALAD

Serve this herbed salad with polenta squares or rice. Adding simply steamed greens as a side dish completes the meal.

2 cups gluten
1 cup plain soymilk or Rice Dream beverage
1 teaspoon tahini
1 teaspoon umeboshi paste
2 tablespoons sake or white wine
4 radishes, sliced into thin rounds
¼ cup sliced ripe black olives
Boston or bibb lettuce to use as a bed for the salad*

MARINADE
2 cups water
2 tablespoons wine vinegar
1 tablespoon sesame oil
1 recipe Savory Seasoning Blend (page 21)

DRESSING
½ cup prepared mayonnaise
2 tablespoons reserved gluten marinade

CALLS FOR:
Gluten

SUGGESTED COOKING METHOD:
Baking

YIELD:
6 servings

ತಿ **About Vinegars**

Brown rice vinegar, unrefined malt and cider vinegars, and balsamic vinegar are superior in flavor and quality to the refined white varieties.

* Instead of lettuce, you can use steamed greens such as spinach, kale, collards, Swiss chard, or broccoli. To serve, place the seitan salad on a large serving platter and surround with the cooked greens.

1. Cut the gluten into slices and arrange them in a lightly oiled 9-x-13-inch baking dish and set aside. In a small pan, combine the marinade ingredients and bring them to a boil. Pour the hot marinade over the gluten and marinate the slices for 2 hours, turning them over occasionally.
2. Once the gluten is marinated, preheat the oven to 350°F. Drain and reserve the marinade.
3. Combine the soymilk, tahini, umeboshi paste, and sake. Cover the gluten slices with this mixture and place in the oven. Bake for 20–30 minutes, turning the slices once.

4. Transfer the baked seitan to a bowl, cover, and refrigerate. Once chilled, use two forks to pull apart the seitan into small, irregular-shaped pieces. Add the radishes and olives.
5. To make the dressing, blend together the mayonnaise and reserved marinade. Add this to the seitan and vegetables. Toss gently.
6. Arrange the lettuce in a serving bowl or platter, and top with the seitan salad.

SPRING SALAD WITH NEW POTATOES AND SNOW PEAS

CALLS FOR:
Gluten

SUGGESTED COOKING METHOD:
Deep-frying

YIELD:
6 servings

I love the way gluten expands to a golden crispness when it is deep-fried. In this salad, it adds a light, chewy texture to the earthy sweetness of new red potatoes and steamed fresh snow peas.

2 cups gluten
Oil for deep-frying
4 cups boiling water for rinsing deep-fried seitan
1 red onion, sliced into very thin half-rounds
1 celery stalk, cut into ⅛-inch slices
18–20 new red potatoes* (about 2 inches in diameter)
8 ounces snow peas, trimmed and destringed

MUSTARD DRESSING
1 clove garlic, crushed and minced
2 tablespoons umeboshi paste
2½ tablespoons olive oil
2 teaspoons Dijon-style mustard
¼ cup brown rice vinegar
¼ cup apple juice

* If small red potatoes are unavailable, use California white, Yukon Gold, or other potatoes with a high moisture content. Potatoes that are dry and flaky, such as russets, are more suitable for baking.

1. Cut the gluten into ¼-inch slices, then cut each slice into very thin strips. Heat 2–3 inches of oil in a 3- or 4-quart saucepan. When the oil is hot, deep-fry the gluten strips until they are golden (5–8 minutes). Place the strips in a colander and rinse with the boiling water to remove any excess oil. Squeeze the strips, pat them dry, and set aside.

2. To prepare the Mustard Dressing, place the garlic and umeboshi paste in a medium bowl and, using the back of a spoon, combine them well. Add the oil, 1 teaspoon at a time, mixing constantly with a whisk. Gradually add the mustard, vinegar, and apple juice. Whisk the dressing until it is thick and creamy.

3. Add the onion and celery to the dressing. Marinate at room temperature.

4. Peel a narrow strip of skin from the potatoes to prevent them from bursting, then gently boil them in lightly salted water until they are tender. Drain the potatoes, cut them in half, and cool.

5. Place the snow peas in a colander and rinse them with fresh water. Bring 4 quarts of water to a boil. Gradually pour some of the boiling water over the snow peas, then shake the colander to rotate the peas. Repeat with the rest of the water. Wait 1 to 2 minutes, then refresh the peas in cold water. Drain, cover, and refrigerate.

6. Carefully add the potatoes and seitan strips to the marinating vegetables. Cover and refrigerate for at least 20 minutes, then set aside at room temperature for 10 minutes.

7. To serve, arrange the snow peas around the edge of a platter and place the salad in the center, or mix the snow peas right into the salad before serving.

LARGE-SHELL MACARONI SALAD WITH ALMOND AND PIMIENTO DRESSING

CALLS FOR:
Seitan cubes

SUGGESTED
COOKING METHOD:
None

YIELD:
6 servings

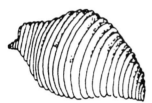

If you use precooked macaroni and green beans, and a dressing that has been prepared in advance, this unusual "hearty" salad will be a pleasure to prepare as well as eat. Add a little brown rice syrup to the dressing for a sweeter taste.

2 cups (about 1 pound) seitan cubes (½ inch)
12 ounces large shell or spiral macaroni
2 pounds green beans, trimmed and cut into 2-inch pieces
½ cup dulse sea vegetable
1 cup finely minced onion

ALMOND-PIMIENTO DRESSING
½ cup whole almonds
3 tablespoons olive oil
¼ cup brown rice vinegar
½ cup freshly squeezed orange juice
¼ cup pimiento strips
1 teaspoon tarragon
½ teaspoon sea salt
2 teaspoons brown rice syrup, optional

1. Cook the pasta al dente according to package directions. Drain in a colander and rinse with cold water. Drain again and place in a tightly covered bowl. Refrigerate.
2. Steam the beans until they are just tender and bright green in color. Drain them in a colander, then plunge them into cold water to stop the cooking and set the bright color. Drain again and place them on a cloth towel to dry.
3. To prepare the dressing, first heat the almonds in a dry skillet over medium-low heat, stirring them constantly. Place the hot roasted almonds on a clean work surface and crush them coarsely with a rolling pin. Transfer the almonds to a mixing bowl, add the oil, and coat the pieces well. Blend in the vinegar, orange juice, pimientos, tarragon, and salt.

4. Combine the dressing with the chilled pasta. Add the green beans, dulse, onion, seitan cubes, and brown rice syrup (if using). Mix together gently and refrigerate.

5. Allow the salad to chill 1–1½ hours before serving. While the salad chills, gently toss it a few times to allow the flavors to blend.

FRAGRANT CHINESE PASTA SALAD

CALLS FOR:
Gluten

SUGGESTED
COOKING METHOD:
Deep-frying

YIELD:
6 servings

Red bell pepper and bright blanched greens give this salad a dash of color.
For additional flavorful crunch, add a cup of blanched mung bean sprouts.

½ cup gluten, cut into ¼-inch slices
Oil for deep-frying
8 cups boiling water (4 cups for rinsing seitan,
4 cups for cooking greens)
2 fresh or dried shiitake mushrooms
2 cups finely chopped greens (kale, collard or mustard
greens, or broccoli rabe)
17-ounce package Chinese rice noodles
1 red bell pepper, sliced very thin

SEASONING BROTH
2 tablespoons water
2 tablespoons natural soy sauce
2 slices fresh ginger, ⅛ inch thick

FRAGRANT SWEET-AND-SOUR DRESSING
1 cup water
½ cup white miso
3 tablespoons brown rice vinegar
2 tablespoons sesame oil
2 tablespoons honey
1½ teaspoons toasted (dark) sesame oil
½ teaspoon black pepper

1. Heat 2–3 inches of oil in a 3- or 4-quart saucepan. Deep-fry the gluten slices until they are golden and crispy. Transfer the slices to a colander and rinse with 4 cups of boiling water to remove any excess oil. Squeeze the slices firmly, then cut them into ¼-inch strips. Set aside.

2. Next, prepare the dressing. Using a fork or spoon, mix the water and miso together in a small saucepan until smooth. Add the remaining dressing ingredients and combine well. Heat over medium heat. Just before the mixture begins to boil, remove the pan from the heat.

3. Remove and discard the woody stem from each shiitake mushroom and cut the caps into ⅛-inch slices. (If using the dried variety, you must first reconstitute them. Simply soak the mushrooms in ½ cup warm water for about 20 minutes.) Set the slices aside.

4. Plunge the greens into the remaining boiling water for 3 minutes, then into cold water. Drain and squeeze the greens to remove excess water, then set aside.

5. Boil the rice noodles until they are just tender. Drain them immediately, then rinse briefly with cold water.

6. To make the Seasoning Broth, combine the water, soy sauce, and ginger slices in a saucepan and bring to a boil. Add the seitan and mushrooms, then reduce the heat and simmer for about 5 minutes, stirring frequently for even-coating. Continue to simmer until no liquid remains. Remove the ginger slices.

7. Add the seitan-mushroom mixture to the noodles. Also add the cooked greens, bell pepper, and dressing. Lightly toss and serve.

TWO-BEAN SALAD WITH HICKORY-FLAVORED STRIPS

CALLS FOR:
Seitan strips

SUGGESTED COOKING METHOD:
Pan-simmering

YIELD:
4–6 servings

Navy beans and green beans combine with hickory-flavored seitan in this new version of an old favorite.

1 cup (about ½ pound) seitan strips (1½ x ¼ inches)
4 cups cooked navy beans or other cooked white beans
¼–½ medium red onion, diced
1½ cups green beans, trimmed and cut into 1½-inch lengths

HICKORY BROTH
1 clove garlic, crushed and minced
¼ cup water
2 teaspoons barley miso or brown rice miso
2 teaspoons natural soy sauce
2 teaspoons liquid hickory-smoke flavoring
½ teaspoon sesame oil
½ teaspoon brown rice vinegar or apple cider vinegar

PARSLEY DRESSING
2 cloves garlic, crushed and minced
1 tablespoon plus 2 teaspoons umeboshi paste
2 tablespoons olive oil or sesame oil
3 tablespoons brown rice vinegar or apple cider vinegar
2 teaspoons Dijon-style mustard
½ teaspoon celery seeds
2 tablespoons water
½ cup minced parsley

1. Make the dressing by combining the garlic and umeboshi paste in a small bowl. Add the oil slowly, mixing continuously to blend well. Add the vinegar, mustard, celery seeds, and water. Blend until smooth. Add the parsley and let the dressing rest for 5 minutes to let the flavors blend.
2. In a medium saucepan, bring all the Hickory Broth ingredients to a boil. Add the seitan and reduce the heat to

medium, stirring frequently until all the broth is absorbed (5–8 minutes). Transfer the seitan to a plate, cover, and refrigerate until chilled.

3. Heat the beans in a medium saucepan, drain, and add them to the dressing along with the onion. Refrigerate until chilled. While the beans are chilling, mix them occasionally to evenly coat with dressing.

4. Steam the green beans until they are tender and bright green in color. Drain them in a colander, then plunge them into cold water to stop the cooking and set the bright color. Drain the beans again, then pat them dry. Cover and refrigerate.

5. When the marinated navy beans are cool, add the seitan strips and half the green beans. To serve, place the bean salad on a platter and surround with the remaining green beans.

WATERCRESS AND WHITE MUSHROOM SALAD WITH GOLDEN SEITAN STRIPS

CALLS FOR:
Gluten

SUGGESTED COOKING METHOD:
Deep-frying

YIELD:
6 servings

Dark green watercress, white mushroom slices, and golden strips of seitan are combined in this perfect side-dish salad that is easy to make.

½ cup gluten
Oil for deep-frying
8 cups boiling water (4 cups for rinsing
deep-fried seitan, 4 cups for blanching watercress)
2 large or 3 small bunches watercress
8 ounces white mushrooms, cut into ⅛-inch slices

CREAMY UMEBOSHI DRESSING
1½ tablespoons umeboshi paste
½ cup plain soymilk or Rice Dream beverage
2 teaspoons sesame oil or safflower oil
½ teaspoon brown rice vinegar
1 teaspoon chopped fresh dill
1 teaspoon chopped fresh thyme

1. In a small bowl, prepare the dressing by adding the soymilk a little at a time to the umeboshi paste. Mix well with a fork or whisk. Add the oil, brown rice vinegar, dill, and thyme, and continue to mix. Refrigerate.

2. Cut the gluten into thin ½-inch-long strips. Heat 2–3 inches of oil in a 3- or 4-quart saucepan. Deep-fry the gluten strips until they are golden (3–5 minutes). Transfer the strips to a colander and rinse with 4 cups of boiling water to remove any excess oil. Squeeze the strips, pat them dry, and set aside.

3. In the remaining boiling water, blanch the watercress, one bunch at a time, for 30 seconds. Immediately plunge each bunch into cold water, drain, and squeeze firmly. Cut the watercress into 2-inch pieces and set aside.

4. Place the sliced mushrooms in the colander and pour the remaining boiling water over them. Toss the mushrooms, wait 30 seconds, then rinse them with cold water. Drain the mushrooms well.

5. In a large bowl, combine the seitan strips, watercress, and mushrooms. Shake the dressing, add it to the bowl, and toss gently.*

6. Serve the salad at room temperature.

---

* It is best to add the dressing just before serving. For best results, the dressing and vegetables should be at room temperature before you combine them.

CINNAMON-CITRUS WILD RICE SALAD

CALLS FOR:
Seitan cubes

SUGGESTED
COOKING METHOD:
Broiling

YIELD:
6 servings

The aromatic sweetness of this rice salad makes it delicious in any season. It's a perfect hot-weather main dish or a side dish to complement a festive holiday meal.

2 cups (about 1 pound) seitan cubes (¾ inch)
2 tangerines, peeled and sectioned
¼ cup mirin
¾ cup raisins
½ cup water
2 cups cooked wild rice
2 cups cooked long-grain brown rice
¼ cup minced red onion (about ½ medium onion)
1½ cups diced celery (about 2 stalks)
4 radishes, sliced into thin rounds
Boston or leaf lettuce to use as a bed for the salad

CINNAMON-CITRUS DRESSING
2 tablespoons toasted (dark) sesame oil
1 teaspoon cinnamon
4–5 tablespoons natural soy sauce
6 tablespoons freshly squeezed orange juice
5 tablespoons freshly squeezed lemon juice

1. To make the dressing, begin by whisking together the oil, cinnamon, and soy sauce in a small bowl. Continue to whisk while adding the orange and lemon juice 1 tablespoon at a time. Store the dressing in a covered jar in the refrigerator. Shake well before using.
2. In a small pot, simmer the tangerine sections in the mirin for 2–3 minutes. Transfer the tangerines to a bowl and refrigerate.
3. In the same pot, boil the raisins in the ½ cup water for 2–3 minutes. Remove the pot from the heat and set it aside so the raisins continue to absorb the water as they cool to room temperature.

4. Place the seitan cubes on a lightly oiled baking sheet and broil about 3 inches from the heat source for 1–2 minutes on each side. Set them aside to cool.
5. In a large bowl, combine the wild rice, brown rice, seitan cubes, onion, celery, radishes, raisins, and the dressing. Mix together lightly.
6. Spoon the rice salad onto a bed of lettuce and garnish with the mirin-flavored tangerine sections.

ESCAROLE AND SEITAN SALAD WITH ANCHOVY-TARRAGON VINAIGRETTE

CALLS FOR:
Gluten

SUGGESTED COOKING METHOD:
Boiling

YIELD:
6 servings

This escarole salad with dumpling-style seitan is accented by the rich flavors of anchovies, tarragon, and oil-cured black olives. A garnish of toasted nori sea vegetable adds the finishing touch to this quickly prepared green salad.

½ cup gluten
2 cups water
2-inch piece kombu
½ red onion, sliced into thin rings
½ teaspoon finely minced lemon zest
1 sheet nori sea vegetable
1 large head escarole or chickory,
cleaned and torn into bite-size pieces
⅓ cup oil-cured black olives

ANCHOVY-TARRAGON VINAIGRETTE
8 anchovy fillets
2 tablespoons freshly squeezed lemon juice
2 tablespoons sesame oil
½ cup plus 2 tablespoons olive oil
2 tablespoons brown rice vinegar
1 teaspoon dry mustard
1½ teaspoons tarragon
2 garlic cloves, crushed

1. Prepare the vinaigrette. Using a fork, mash the anchovies in a small bowl. Mix in the lemon juice. In a separate bowl, combine the sesame oil and olive oil. Alternately whisk the oil and the vinegar, 1 teaspoon at a time, into the bowl with the anchovy-lemon mixture. Whisk in the tarragon and garlic. Cover the dressing and set it aside for at least 20 minutes to allow the flavors to blend at room temperature.

2. In a small saucepan, bring the water and kombu to a boil. Break off tiny pieces of gluten and drop them into the water one by one. Cook these "dumplings" for 10–12 minutes. Transfer the cooked dumplings to a colander and set aside to drain.

3. Place ¾ cup of the salad dressing in a large bowl along with the onion and lemon zest. Add the dumplings while they are still hot. Refrigerate until just chilled, stirring occasionally.

4. While the dumplings are chilling, toast the nori by holding it in one hand and passing it back and forth over a medium-high flame. Tear the toasted nori sheet into irregular bite-size pieces.

5. Just before serving, add the escarole to the marinated seitan and onions. Toss lightly and add dressing to taste. Garnish with olives and nori.

GINGERED BROCCOLI RABE WITH TINY CROQUETTES

CALLS FOR:
Ground seitan

This is an easy way to use a small amount of seitan as an accent for greens. If broccoli rabe is not available, try mustard greens, kale, collard greens, or steamed broccoli flowerets instead. They are delicious variations.

SUGGESTED
COOKING METHOD:
Deep-frying

½ cup ground seitan (about ¼ pound)
½ cup cooked brown rice (medium soft)
1 teaspoon arrowroot
Oil for deep-frying
1 recipe Hearty Seasoning Blend (page 21), or to taste
1 bunch broccoli rabe (up to 1 pound)

YIELD:
6 servings

GINGER DRESSING
3 tablespoons brown rice vinegar
3 teaspoons natural soy sauce
¾ teaspoon ginger root juice*

* Grate 1-inch piece of peeled fresh ginger and squeeze to extract juice.

1. To make the dressing, simply combine the ingredients in a small bowl, and adjust to taste. Cover the dressing and set aside at room temperature.
2. To make croquettes, combine seitan, rice, arrowroot, and Hearty Seasoning Blend (if using) in a medium bowl. Form the balls, using about 1 teaspoon of mixture for each ball.
3. Heat 2–3 inches of oil in a 3- or 4-quart saucepan and deep-fry the balls until they are brown and crispy. Remove them from the oil and place on paper towels.
4. Boil the broccoli rabe until it is bright green in color (about 5 minutes). Plunge it immediately into cold water to stop the cooking and set the color. Transfer the rabe to a colander to drain, then squeeze gently to remove excess water. Cut the greens crosswise into 1½-inch lengths, then separate the pieces.
5. Place the broccoli rabe in a salad bowl, add the seitan croquettes and dressing, and toss gently.

CONFETTI RICE SALAD WITH CREAMY CHIVE DRESSING

CALLS FOR:
Seitan strips

SUGGESTED COOKING METHOD:
None

YIELD:
6 servings

Using precooked brown rice makes this colorful salad quick to prepare. Red peppers, yellow summer squash, and green scallions add splashes of color to this flavorful dish.

1–2 cups (½–1 pound) seitan strips (½ inch wide)
5 cups cooked short or long-grain brown rice,
at room temperature
2–4 tablespoons natural soy sauce
2–3 tablespoons lemon juice
½–1 teaspoon wasabi powder*
1 cup diced sweet red bell pepper
2 cucumbers, diced into ½–¾-inch pieces
2 scallions, sliced very thin
1 small yellow summer squash, cut into thin matchsticks
Green leaf lettuce or another crispy green
to use as a bed for the salad

CREAMY CHIVE DRESSING
1 tablespoon white miso
1 tablespoon umeboshi paste
½ cup plain soymilk or Rice Dream beverage
4 teaspoons tahini
¼ cup water
2 tablespoons lemon juice, or to taste
¼ cup minced fresh chives

❧ About Whole Grains

Due to their healthful and wholesome nature, unrefined whole grains are suggested for the recipes in this book. Grains such as whole wheat and brown rice are considerably more nourishing than refined grains like white flour and white rice. The naturally occurring bran and fiber in whole grains is essential for optimum health.

* Wasabi (horseradish) powder is available in natural foods stores, Asian markets, and some supermarkets.

1. Place the cooked rice in a large bowl and top with the seitan strips. Combine the soy sauce, lemon juice, and wasabi powder, then pour it over the rice and seitan. Mix together carefully to keep the seitan strips from breaking.
2. To make the dressing, place the miso and umeboshi in a small bowl. Mix in the soymilk a little at a time to form a smooth paste. Add the tahini. Stir in enough water to

achieve the desired consistency, and add lemon juice to taste. Mix in the chives and combine well.

3. To assemble the salad, add the bell peppers, cucumbers, scallions, and squash to the rice mixture along with ¾ cup of the dressing. Mix together well.

4. Place the rice salad on a bed of lettuce, garnish with the squash matchsticks, and top with the remaining dressing.

HOT WILTED SPINACH SALAD WITH SESAME-CHILI BRAISED SEITAN AND BELL PEPPERS

CALLS FOR:
Seitan cutlets

SUGGESTED COOKING METHOD:
Pan-simmering

YIELD:
6 servings

The combination of dramatic, bold flavors and rich taste is the keynote of this salad that features spicy Thai red-curry paste. Serve this exotic dish along with whole wheat pita toast and a smooth, puréed soup, such as Golden Squash Potage (page 64).

6 chilled seitan cutlets (about 1½ pounds)
4 tablespoons coconut milk
2 tablespoons honey or brown rice syrup
1 teaspoon Thai red-curry paste*
3 tablespoons minced fresh cilantro leaves
1 medium Vidalia onion, sliced into thin half moons**
10–16 ounces fresh spinach, washed and patted dry
1 large orange, red, or yellow bell pepper,
sliced into ¼-inch strips

MARINADE
3 tablespoons sesame oil
1 tablespoon toasted (dark) sesame oil
½ cup rice wine vinegar
Freshly squeezed juice from 1 lime
½ teaspoon garlic granules
¼ teaspoon black pepper

* Available in Asian markets.
**Can substitute Spanish onion for Vidalia onion.

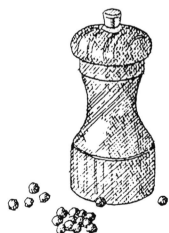

1. In a medium bowl, combine the marinade ingredients and mix well. Slice the seitan cutlets into thin strips (1-x-2-x-⅛ inch). Add the strips to the marinade, toss well, and set aside for 20–30 minutes, turning frequently.
2. In a 10-inch frying pan, combine the coconut milk, honey, curry paste, and cilantro. Heat for 3 minutes over medium heat.
3. Reserving the marinade, remove the seitan strips and add them to the pan along with the onions. Cover and simmer for 5 minutes. Turn the seitan and onions, add the reserved marinade, then cover and simmer 5 minutes more. Uncover and continue to simmer until the sauce is reduced by about half.
4. While the seitan is simmering, tear the spinach into bite-size pieces and place in a salad bowl along with the bell pepper.
5. Add the hot seitan with the sauce to the salad bowl and toss carefully. The heat will cause the spinach to wilt.
6. Serve the salad hot or at room temperature.

7

SIDE DISHES

*One cannot think well, love well, sleep well,
if one has not dined well.*

—Virginia Woolf (1882–1941)
A Room of One's Own

Side dishes provide an opportunity to include a wonderful combination of flavors and textures that enhances other foods in a meal. A very simple meal of whole grains or whole grain pasta and steamed vegetables will be complemented by an interesting seitan side dish.

Most of the recipes offered in this chapter are fairly simple to make, and many are suitable to prepare as entrées as well as side dishes. Szechuan-Style Sweet-and-Sour Cubes (page 104), Baked Buttercup Treasure Chest (page 110), and Seitan and Green Beans in Mustard Sauce (page 122) are just a sample of the many flavors, textures, and cooking styles presented in this section.

SZECHUAN-STYLE SWEET-AND-SOUR CUBES

CALLS FOR:
Seitan cubes

SUGGESTED COOKING METHOD:
Deep-frying
or broiling

YIELD:
4 servings

Crispy cubes of seitan are immersed in a hot sweet-and-sour sauce then dotted with chunks of pineapple. Perfect to serve over rice or noodles.

2 cups (about 1 pound) seitan cubes (1 inch)
Oil for deep-frying
1 can (20 ounces) unsweetened pineapple chunks with juice
2 tablespoons arrowroot flour
¼ cup water
½ teaspoon natural soy sauce
A few drops Chinese hot pepper oil, or Tabasco sauce
2 teaspoons brown rice vinegar or cider vinegar
2 teaspoons brown rice syrup, barley malt syrup, or honey
2 scallions, cut lengthwise into 2-inch strips
½ medium red bell pepper, cut into 2-inch squares
½ medium green bell pepper, cut into 2-inch squares

1. Heat 2–3 inches of oil in a 3- or 4-quart saucepan. Without overcrowding the pan, deep-fry the seitan cubes until crispy on all sides (3–5 minutes).* Place the cubes on absorbent paper towels to remove any excess oil.
2. Drain the pineapple, reserving the juice. Add enough water to the juice to total 1½ cups of liquid. Heat the juice in a large saucepan over medium-low heat.
3. While the juice is heating, dissolve the arrowroot in ¼ cup of water. Add the soy sauce, pepper oil, vinegar, and syrup to the arrowroot. Stir this mixture into the hot pineapple juice and stir until the sauce is thick and clear (2–5 minutes). Add the peppers, pineapple chunks, seitan cubes, and scallions, and heat thoroughly. Be careful not to overcook this dish or the sauce will become watery.
4. Serve with rice or noodles.

* You can broil the seitan cubes instead of deep-frying them. Simply place the cubes on a lightly oiled baking sheet, and broil them until they are browned and crispy on all sides (about 6 minutes). While the cubes are broiling, watch them closely so they don't burn.

BAKED COUNTRY-STYLE PATTIES WITH GRATED APPLES AND SAUERKRAUT

These spicy, sausage-flavored patties are delicious when baked with apples and sauerkraut. This combination is a hearty companion to steaming brown rice or crusty whole wheat sourdough bread.

CALLS FOR:
Ground seitan

SUGGESTED COOKING METHOD:
Baking

YIELD:
12 small patties

2 cups ground seitan (about 1 pound)
4 cups (32-ounces) naturally fermented sauerkraut
2 cups water
2 tablespoons whole wheat pastry flour
¼ cup chickpea flour
1 recipe Spicy Seasoning Blend (page 21)
3 tablespoons sesame oil
1 tart apple (Granny Smith), unpeeled

1. Drain the sauerkraut and squeeze it gently to remove the excess brine. Place the sauerkraut and water in a bowl, and let it soak about 15 minutes to remove some of the salt.
2. While the sauerkraut is soaking, prepare the seitan patties. In a large bowl, combine the seitan, pastry flour, chickpea flour, and Spicy Seasoning Blend. Form the mixture into 12 small patties (1½–2 inches in diameter).
3. Preheat the oven to 300°F. Heavily coat a medium oven-proof casserole dish with cooking oil and set it aside.
4. In a heavy skillet, heat the sesame oil over medium heat. Add the seitan patties and cook them until well-browned (5–7 minutes on each side).
5. Grate the apple into a medium bowl and set aside. Reserving the soaking water, drain and firmly squeeze the sauerkraut, then combine it with the grated apple.
6. Place the seitan patties in the prepared casserole dish. Cover the patties with the apple-sauerkraut mixture and half of the reserved soaking water.
7. Cover and bake the patties until they are heated through (45–60 minutes). Serve hot.

FILLED NOODLE NESTS

CALLS FOR:
Seitan strips

SUGGESTED
COOKING METHOD:
Pan-simmering

YIELD:
6 servings

This delightful dish is composed of seitan and vegetables that are served in a nest of deep-fried noodles. Red Simmered Seitan (page 107) is another interesting filling for these nests, although, just about any style seitan will do.

2 cups (about 1 pound) seitan strips (2 x ½ x ⅛ inches)
2½ tablespoons arrowroot
¼ cup water for dissolving arrowroot
2 tablespoons natural soy sauce
1 tablespoon mirin
1 teaspoon grated fresh ginger root
1 tablespoon sesame oil
½ pound snow peas, trimmed and destringed
1 can (8 ounces) sliced water chestnuts
1½ cups stock or water

NOODLE NESTS
8 ounces whole wheat spaghetti or linguini,
cooked al dente and chilled
Oil for deep-frying

1. To prepare the noodle nests, heat 3 inches of oil in a 3- or 4-quart saucepan. Immerse ½ cup of noodles (be sure they are chilled and dry) in the hot oil, and keep them submerged with chopsticks or tongs. Hold the noodles against the sides of the pot to form the shape of a nest. After about a minute, the shape should be set. Release the noodles, turn the nest over, and cook until crispy and golden. Place on absorbent paper towels to remove any excess oil.
2. To prepare the filling, first dissolve the arrowroot in ¼ cup of water. Add the soy sauce, mirin, and ginger, and set aside.
3. Heat the sesame oil in a large skillet or wok over high heat. Add the seitan strips and quickly stir-fry them until browned and crispy (5–7 minutes). Add the snow peas and water chestnuts, and continue to stir-fry over high

heat. When the vegetables are thoroughly heated, add the stock and arrowroot mixture. Heat and stir until the sauce is translucent.

4. Arrange the noodle nests on a platter or individual plates and fill with the seitan-vegetable sauce.

RED SIMMERED SEITAN

CALLS FOR:
Seitan pieces

SUGGESTED
COOKING METHOD:
Pan-simmering

YIELD:
6 servings

I love the fragrance of toasted sesame oil mixed with anise. This traditional Chinese preparation adapts beautifully to seitan, and is perfect to use in Filled Noodle Nests (page 106).

4 cups (about 2 pounds) seitan pieces (1½ x 2½ inches)
3 tablespoons toasted (dark) sesame oil
2 cloves garlic
3 tablespoons natural soy sauce
3 tablespoons mirin
8 cloves Chinese star anise*
2 tablespoons brown rice syrup
¼ teaspoon Chinese hot pepper oil
2 cups water
2 scallions, slivered for garnish

* One section of a "star" is considered one clove.

1. In a heavy pot with a cover, heat the sesame oil over medium heat. Add the seitan pieces and brown them until crispy (5–7 minutes on each side).
2. Add the remaining ingredients to the pot and lower the heat. Cover and simmer for 2 hours, turning the pieces every 20 minutes for even cooking.
3. Transfer the seitan to a serving bowl and top with the simmered sauce. Garnish with scallions and serve warm or cold.

PAN-SIMMERED CUTLETS IN A SAUCE OF SUN-DRIED TOMATOES WITH YELLOW BELL PEPPER AND OIL-CURED OLIVES

CALLS FOR:
Seitan cutlets

SUGGESTED
COOKING METHOD:
**Pan-simmering
or oven-braising**

YIELD:
6 servings

You can almost feel the warm sunshine and gentle Mediterranean breezes with every bite of these aromatic seitan cutlets. The unique tomato-based sauce is unbelieveably simple to prepare.

6–8 seitan cutlets (1½–2 pounds)
½ medium onion, minced fine
1 large yellow bell pepper,
seeded and cut into bite-size pieces
1 tablespoon olive oil
2 tablespoons minced fresh parsley, or 2 teaspoons dried
½ cup whole oil-cured black olives
Fresh parsley for garnish

SAUCE
1 cup sun-dried tomato halves
1 cup boiling water
4 cloves garlic
1 comice pear, peeled, cored, and cut into 1-inch chunks
1 teaspoon ground coriander
¼ teaspoon black pepper
3 tablespoons olive oil

1. First, prepare the sauce. In a small bowl, cover the sun-dried tomatoes with the boiling water. Allow the tomatoes to soak 15 minutes. Drain the tomatoes and set aside, reserving the liquid.
2. In a food processor or blender, purée the garlic and pear. Add the soaked tomatoes and continue to blend the ingredients while adding the reserved soaking liquid a little at a time. Add the coriander, black pepper, and olive

oil, and continue to purée the ingredients until smooth. Set aside.

3. Heat 1 tablespoon of olive oil in a heavy skillet over medium heat. Add the onions and sauté them until translucent and beginning to brown (about 2 minutes).

4. Add the cutlets to the skillet (do not overlap) and cook them about 10 minutes on each side. Add the bell pepper. Spoon the reserved sauce evenly over the seitan. Shake the pan gently from side to side, causing the sauce to move between the cutlets to the bottom of the pan. Top with the olives.

5. Cover the skillet and simmer the cutlets and sauce over low heat for 20–30 minutes.

6. Garnish the cutlets with fresh parsley before serving.

Variation

To oven-braise this dish, first heat the olive oil in a flameproof baking dish over medium heat. Add the onions and sauté them until they are translucent and beginning to brown. Add the cutlets, bell pepper, sauce, and olives. Cover the baking dish and place in a preheated 350°F oven. Remove the cover after 20 minutes and continue to braise the cutlets in the sauce for another 10 minutes. Garnish with parsley before serving.

BAKED BUTTERCUP TREASURE CHEST

CALLS FOR:
Seitan cubes

SUGGESTED
COOKING METHOD:
Baking

YIELD:
6 servings

Provide your family and friends with a real treasure in this buttercup squash, baked whole and filled with onion, seitan, and a little seasoned stock. One of the beauties of this dish is that it can be assembled and refrigerated up to eight hours before it is baked. (Additional baking time will be needed if the squash is chilled.)

2 cups (about 1 pound) seitan cubes (1 inch)
1 medium buttercup squash with a flat bottom
1 medium onion, diced into ½-inch pieces
2 teaspoons minced fresh parsley
¼ cup seasoned stock

1. Preheat the oven to 375°F.
2. Scrub the squash and cut off the top to create a lid about 5 inches in diameter. Scoop out the seeds and either discard them, or save them for roasting or planting. Scrape out some of the squash from inside the lid (so the squash will hold more filling), chop it, and place in a large bowl.
3. Using a small knife and/or metal spoon, carefully trim away the inner walls of the squash to a ¼-inch thickness. Chop the scooped-out squash and place it in the bowl containing the other chopped squash. Mix in the seitan, onion, and parsley. Add the stock and mix the ingredients together well.
4. Fill the hollowed-out squash with this seitan-vegetable mixture and replace the lid. Secure the cover by tying a string around the entire squash.
5. Place the filled squash on a baking sheet. Bake the squash until it is tender and a fork is able to penetrate its skin easily (45–60 minutes).
6. Transfer the baked squash to a serving plate. To serve, remove the string and lid, and scoop out steaming portions.

ENCHILADAS IN CREAM SAUCE

CALLS FOR:
Ground seitan

SUGGESTED
COOKING METHOD:
Baking

YIELD:
6 enchiladas

This enchilada casserole is easy to prepare and requires only twenty-five minutes of baking. The addition of a dairy-free cream sauce makes this preparation unusually delicious and healthful.

2 cups ground seitan (about 1 pound)
1 cup prepared tomato sauce
1 teaspoon chili powder, or combination of:
½ teaspoon cumin, ¼ teaspoon cayenne pepper,
and ¼ teaspoon garlic granules
6 soft corn tortillas

NONDAIRY CREAM SAUCE
1½ teaspoons kuzu or arrowroot
½ cup plain soymilk or Rice Dream beverage
¾ teaspoon tahini
½ teaspoons umeboshi plum vinegar (ume-su)*

* Available in natural foods stores.

1. Preheat the oven to 350°F. Oil a 10-inch-square baking dish and set aside.
2. First, prepare the sauce. In a small saucepan, dissolve the kuzu in 2 tablespoons of soymilk. Add the rest of the soymilk, tahini, and vinegar. Over medium heat, stir the sauce constantly until it is thick and creamy. Remove the pan from the heat and set it aside.
3. Next, make the enchilada filling by combining the seitan, tomato sauce, and chili powder.
4. Spoon 2 heaping tablespoons of the filling onto the center of a tortilla. Fold the sides over and place the tortilla seam side down in the prepared baking dish. Spoon 1 tablespoon of the cream sauce over each tortilla. Cover the dish and bake for 25 minutes.
5. Serve the enchiladas hot.

SEITAN SIAM

CALLS FOR:
Seitan cutlets

SUGGESTED
COOKING METHOD:
Pan-simmering

YIELD:
6 servings

Freshly steamed greens complement this fiery dish beautifully. As Seitan Siam is very spicy, you might want to reduce the amount of chilies.

6 seitan cutlets (about 1½ pounds),
cut into 12 half-inch-thick squares
1 can (14 ounces) coconut milk, unshaken
2 tablespoons toasted (dark) sesame oil
4 cloves garlic, crushed and minced
1–2 teaspoons finely minced hot chili peppers
1 teaspoon minced fresh ginger
2 tablespoons natural soy sauce
2 tablespoons minced fresh coriander leaves
2 tablespoons minced fresh mint
3 ounces snow peas, trimmed and blanched

> **🍃 About Soy Sauce**
>
> *Tamari and shoyu are natural soy sauces and are preferred over the commercial varieties found in most supermarkets. Products made by Westbrae, Erewhon, Eden, and Ohsawa America are free from chemicals and preservatives, and are superior in body and flavor to most commercial brands.*

1. First, separate the coconut milk. In every can of coconut milk, the thick milk rises to the top, while the thin milk stays on the bottom. To separate, simply scoop out the thick portion and place it in a small bowl. Measure ½ cup of this thick milk and place in a cup or small bowl. In another bowl, place ⅓ cup of the thin milk. Set these milks aside.
2. Heat the oil in a large heavy skillet over medium heat. Add the garlic, chiles, and ginger, and sauté them for 3 minutes. Add the seitan and soy sauce.
3. Cover the skillet and brown the seitan on one side (about 10 minutes). Turn the seitan over, add the coriander, mint, and thick and thin coconut milks. Cover and simmer for about 10 minutes.
4. Spoon the spicy seitan into a serving bowl and garnish with snow peas. Enjoy with hot rice or pasta.

ONION-CARAWAY BALLS WITH SAUERKRAUT

Caraway seeds and minced onion are kneaded into the gluten, which is then formed into balls and deep-fried. The puffed golden balls are combined with sauerkraut to create a perfect cold-weather meal.

2 cups gluten
2 tablespoons natural soy sauce
⅝ cup finely diced onion
1 tablespoon caraway seeds
Oil for deep-frying
2 cups drained, chopped, tightly packed sauerkraut
1¼ cups water

1. Run hot water over the gluten to soften it. Place the gluten on a clean work surface and pat, pound, and stretch it to a ½-inch thickness. Sprinkle the soy sauce, onion, and caraway seeds over the surface of the gluten, fold it in half, and let it rest a few minutes. (As you work, puncture any air bubbles that develop in the gluten with a skewer or sharp knife.)

2. Knead the onions and caraway seeds into the gluten by repeatedly folding the gluten in half and pressing down firmly. Pull, stretch, and twist the gluten as much as necessary to embed the onion and caraway seeds firmly in the gluten. (Some of the onion and seeds may fall out, but most of them will stick to the gluten.) Let the gluten rest another few minutes.

3. Tightly roll the gluten into a cylinder. Cut the cylinder into 2-inch slices, then roll the slices into small cylinders. Slice the small cylinders into 1-inch pieces and set aside.

4. Heat 2–3 inches of oil in a 3- or 4-quart saucepan. Without overcrowding the pot, add the gluten pieces one by one. Using chopsticks or a fork, keep the gluten completely submerged for the first 10 seconds (for even cooking). Deep-fry the pieces until the edges turn light golden in

CALLS FOR:
Gluten

SUGGESTED COOKING METHODS:
Deep-frying, then pan-simmering

YIELD:
4–6 servings

color (about 3 minutes on each side). Place on absorbent paper towels to remove any excess oil.

5. Heat the sauerkraut and water in a large saucepan over medium heat. Add the seitan balls and combine them with the sauerkraut. Cover and simmer for 15 minutes, stirring occasionally.

6. To serve, transfer to a serving bowl or chafing dish.

EASIEST BARBECUE-FLAVORED BAKED CUTLETS

CALLS FOR:
Gluten

SUGGESTED COOKING METHOD:
Baking

YIELD:
4 servings

The total preparation time for this dish is about forty-five minutes, but I consider it "quick" because it takes only a few minutes to assemble.

2 cups gluten
2¼ cups prepared barbecue sauce

1. Preheat the oven to 400°F.

2. Cut the gluten into 8 slices (½ inch thick). Arrange these cutlets on a lightly oiled baking sheet and place in the oven for 10 minutes. Turn the cutlets over (lightly oil the sheet again under each cutlet before turning them), and bake another 10 minutes.

3. In a medium saucepan, heat the barbecue sauce and add the cutlets. Simmer over medium heat for 15 minutes.

4. Transfer the cutlets to an 8-inch-square shallow baking dish. Cover with the remaining sauce and bake for 10 minutes uncovered. Turn the cutlets and bake a few minutes more until the sauce thickens.

5. Enjoy these cutlets with roasted potatoes, brown rice, and a green salad.

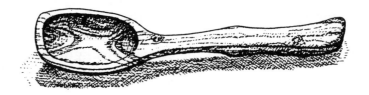

OLD-FASHIONED HICKORY BAKED BEANS

CALLS FOR:
Seitan cutlets

SUGGESTED
COOKING METHODS:
Pan-frying,
then baking

YIELD:
6 servings

In this delicious side dish, navy beans are soaked overnight (or eight hours), then slow baked in a tantalizing hickory-flavored sauce.

2 cups (about 1 pound) sliced seitan cutlets
(about ¼ inch thick)
2 cups dried navy beans
6 cups water for soaking beans
3-inch piece kombu, broken into ¼-inch pieces
½ cup water
4 tablespoons sesame oil
¼ cup tomato paste
¼ cup barley miso or brown rice miso
3 tablespoons barley malt syrup or molasses
1½ teaspoon dry mustard
1 teaspoon liquid hickory-smoke flavoring
1 large onion, diced

1. Spread the beans on a baking sheet and pick through them, discarding any discolored beans or empty shells. Next, place the beans in a colander, rinse them, then transfer them to a medium pot. Add the water and soak 8 hours or overnight.
2. When the beans have finished soaking, drain them and replace the leftover soaking water with an equal amount of fresh water. Add the kombu. Set aside.
3. Preheat the oven to 300°F.
4. To prepare the seasoning mixture, combine ½ cup water with 2 tablespoons sesame oil, the tomato paste, miso, barley malt syrup, mustard, and hickory-smoke flavoring. Add this mixture along with the onions to the beans and water.
5. Heat the remaining 2 tablespoons of sesame oil in a heavy skillet, and pan-fry the seitan until it is crispy.
6. Place the seitan and beans in a narrow-necked stoneware bean pot (or Dutch oven with a tight-fitting cover).

7. Cover and bake the beans for 3–4 hours, stirring them periodically. Check often to make sure they don't dry out. Add a little hot water to the pot as needed.

SWEET-AND-SOUR STRIPS WITH ROMAINE

CALLS FOR:
Seitan cutlets

SUGGESTED COOKING METHOD:
Stir-frying

YIELD:
4 servings

Lightly sweet and sour, this dish is delightfully simple in both its preparation and ingredients.

4 large seitan cutlets (about 1 pound),
cut into ¼-inch-wide strips
1 large head romaine lettuce
1 tablespoon kuzu or arrowroot
¼ cup water
1 tablespoon barley malt syrup
1 tablespoon brown rice vinegar
1 teaspoon natural soy sauce
2 tablespoons sesame oil

1. Cut the lettuce leaves in half lengthwise, then slice the halves crosswise into ½-inch-strips.
2. In a cup or small bowl, dissolve the kuzu in the water, then add the barley malt syrup, vinegar, and soy sauce. Set aside.
3. In a large frying pan or wok, heat the oil and stir-fry the seitan strips until slightly crispy. Add the lettuce and stir-fry until just slightly wilted. Pour the kuzu mixture into the skillet, combining it well with the seitan and lettuce, and cook until the sauce becomes thick and glossy (about 3 minutes).
4. Serve the stir-fried seitan over hot brown rice or noodles.

BREADED SEITAN CUTLETS

CALLS FOR:
Seitan cutlets

SUGGESTED
COOKING METHOD:
Broiling

YIELD:
10 cutlets
(about ¼ inch thick)

Very firm, chilled cutlets will become tender when broiled. This versatile dish can be served with any type of cream, herb, or barbecue sauce.

10 thin seitan cutlets (about 2 pounds)
2 tablespoons arrowroot
⅔ cup plain soymilk or Rice Dream beverage
1½ cups cornmeal
2 tablespoons nutritional yeast
1 teaspoon sesame seeds
¾ teaspoon ground coriander
¾ teaspoon cumin
½ teaspoon garlic granules
½ teaspoon onion flakes
¼ teaspoon celery seeds
⅛ teaspoon white pepper

1. Blot the cutlets with a paper towel to remove surface moisture and set them aside. In a medium bowl, dissolve the arrowroot in the soymilk. In another medium bowl, mix together all the remaining ingredients.
2. Preheat the oven to broil. Lightly oil a baking sheet and set it aside.
3. Dip the cutlets in the soymilk, then roll them in the cornmeal mixture. Press the cornmeal firmly into the cutlets.
4. Place the breaded cutlets on the baking sheet and place them under the broiler about 6 inches from the heat source. Broil for 5–7 minutes, then turn the cutlets over and broil the other side 3–5 minutes.
5. Arrange the cutlets on a serving platter and serve with your favorite sauce.

ROASTED TOMATOES WITH SAVORY STUFFING

CALLS FOR:
Ground seitan

SUGGESTED COOKING METHOD:
Baking

YIELD:
6 stuffed tomatoes

The combination of red and yellow tomatoes adds to the colorful presentation of this dish. Easy to prepare, these stuffed tomatoes take only thirty minutes to bake to a juicy tenderness.

6 medium tomatoes (about 3 inches in diameter)
2 cups ground seitan (about 1 pound)
1 recipe Savory Seasoning Blend (page 21)
6 tablespoons chickpea flour
2 tablespoons whole wheat flour
¼ cup minced fresh parsley
1 teaspoon minced fresh basil
1 clove garlic, crushed and minced
2 teaspoons olive oil or sesame oil

SAUCE
1 teaspoon arrowroot or kuzu
½ cup tomato juice (extracted from tomatoes above)
1 tablespoon natural soy sauce

1. Preheat the oven to 400°F. Lightly oil a baking sheet and set it aside.
2. Slice ¼–½ inch off the top of each tomato. Scoop out the pulp, leaving a thick shell. Place the pulp in a strainer and extract the juice by pressing the pulp against the sides of the strainer with the back of a spoon. Reserve ½ cup of juice for the sauce. Chop the pulp and set it aside.
3. To make the stuffing, combine the seitan, Savory Seasoning Blend, chickpea and whole wheat flours, parsley, basil, garlic, oil, and reserved tomato pulp in a large bowl.
4. Lightly coat the tomato skins with oil, then fill the empty tomatoes with the stuffing, heaping it slightly above the top of each shell.

5. Arrange the stuffed tomatoes on the baking sheet and bake until tender (about 30 minutes). Watch them carefully as they bake so they do not split.
6. When the tomatoes have almost finished baking, prepare the sauce. In a small saucepan, dissolve the arrowroot in the reserved tomato juice. Heat this mixture, stirring until thick. Add the soy sauce.
7. Transfer the cooked tomatoes to a serving platter and top each with a little hot sauce.

CUTLETS ROMANO

These cutlets, which are baked in a tomato sauce with tofu and tahini, can be quick to prepare if you have the breaded cutlets on hand.

1 recipe Breaded Seitan Cutlets (page 117)
8 ounces firm tofu
1 tablespoon umeboshi plum paste
1 tablespoon tahini
2½ cups prepared tomato sauce

CALLS FOR:
Prepared breaded
seitan cutlets

SUGGESTED
COOKING METHOD:
Baking

YIELD:
6–8 servings

1. Preheat the oven to 350°F.
2. In a medium bowl, mash the tofu with a fork. Add the umeboshi paste and tahini, and mix together well.
3. In the bottom of a shallow oiled baking dish, arrange the cutlets in one or two layers and cover with the tomato sauce. Crumble the tofu mixture over the top.
4. Bake uncovered until the tomato sauce is hot and bubbly and the tofu begins to brown (about 20 minutes).
5. Serve the cutlets hot from the oven, accompanied by pasta, polenta, or a vegetable dish.

BAKED CUTLETS WITH ONIONS AND HERBED ALMOND-CRUMB STUFFING

CALLS FOR:
Seitan cutlets

SUGGESTED
COOKING METHOD:
Baking

YIELD:
4–6 servings

Tender, herb-seasoned stuffing with a toasted almond crunch is a delicious addition to these hearty cutlets.

6 seitan cutlets (about 1½ pounds)
1 medium onion, cut crosswise into thin slices
1 cup plain soymilk or Rice Dream beverage
1 tablespoon corn oil or sesame oil

STUFFING
1 cup torn pieces day-old bread, tightly packed
1½ cups coarsely chopped almonds
3 tablespoons dried parsley
1 teaspoon dried rosemary, thyme, or sage
½ teaspoon allspice
¼ teaspoon turmeric

1. Preheat the oven to 400°F. Lightly oil a 1½-quart oven-proof casserole dish and set aside.
2. To make the stuffing, place the bread, almonds, parsley, rosemary, allspice, and turmeric in a blender or food processor, and pulse until coarse crumbs are formed. Set aside.
3. Arrange the seitan cutlets in the bottom of the casserole dish and top with the bread crumb mixture. Place the sliced onions on top of the crumbs.
4. In a small bowl, combine the soymilk and oil. Pour this mixture evenly over the onions. (As you pour, lift each cutlet a little with a fork to make sure the liquid reaches the bottom.)
5. Cover and bake for 30 minutes. Serve immediately.

ROASTED SEITAN WITH RED AND YELLOW PEPPERS IN CHIVE-GARLIC SAUCE

This is one of my favorite seitan dishes. It's easy to prepare, and tastes as good as it looks and smells. Garlic, chives, and a little olive oil enhance the flavor of the seitan and bell peppers.

2 cups (about 1 pound) chilled seitan cubes (2 inches)
2 large red bell peppers, halved and seeded
2 large yellow bell peppers, halved and seeded
1 tablespoon olive oil
¼ cup minced fresh chives

CHIVE-GARLIC SAUCE
6 cloves garlic, crushed and minced
1 tablespoon olive oil
1 cup water
2 tablespoons natural soy sauce
⅓ teaspoon paprika
⅛ teaspoon black pepper

CALLS FOR:
Seitan cubes

SUGGESTED COOKING METHOD:
Baking

YIELD:
4–6 servings

1. Preheat the oven to 450°F.
2. Lightly blot the chilled seitan with paper towels to remove surface moisture. Cut the bell pepper halves into thirds or quarters.
3. Place the seitan and bell peppers in a 1- to 2-inch-deep baking dish, and coat evenly with a thin layer of olive oil. Set aside.
4. To prepare the sauce, combine the garlic, olive oil, water, soy sauce, paprika, and black pepper in a blender. Purée the ingredients, then spoon this mixture evenly over the seitan and peppers.
5. Place in the oven and bake, uncovered, basting the ingredients occasionally with the sauce. Continue to bake until the peppers are tender and the seitan is crispy (20–30 minutes).

6. Remove the dish from the oven and top with half the chives. Baste the seitan and peppers once more, then broil for 1–2 minutes.
7. Transfer the seitan and peppers to a serving bowl, garnish with the remaining chives, and top with the sauce.

SEITAN AND GREEN BEANS IN MUSTARD SAUCE

CALLS FOR:
Seitan cubes

SUGGESTED
COOKING METHODS:
Deep-frying,
then baking

YIELD:
4–6 servings

Juicy golden chunks of crispy batter-fried seitan are paired with fresh green beans in a tangy mustard sauce. A delicious accompaniment to cornbread or muffins.

2 cups (about 1 pound) seitan cubes (¾ inch) .
1 pound green beans, cut crosswise in half,
then lengthwise in half
½ recipe Whole Wheat and Corn Flour Batter (page 31),
chilled
Oil for deep-frying
1 recipe Tangy Mustard Sauce (page 58)

1. Preheat the oven to 350°F.
2. Blanch the green beans and plunge into cold water. Drain, and set aside.
3. Heat 2–3 inches of oil in a 3- or 4-quart saucepan. While the oil is heating, blot the seitan cubes with a paper towel to remove surface moisture, then coat the cubes with batter.
4. Without overcrowding the pan, deep-fry the coated seitan until crispy and golden (5–7 minutes). Place on absorbent paper towels to remove any excess oil.
5. Place the green beans in the bottom of a lightly oiled 2-quart baking dish, and top with the seitan cubes. Pour the Tangy Mustard Sauce evenly over the top.
6. Cover the casserole and bake for 15–20 minutes. Remove the cover and bake 5–10 minutes more.
7. Best served hot.

PRUSSIAN PIROSHKI

Piroshki are savory semi-circles of flaky glazed dough that are filled with seasoned ground seitan. You'll love these turnovers for lunch, dinner, or as part of a picnic feast. Piroshki are also wonderful additions to holiday buffets. Although they require more prepartion than some other dishes, piroshki are definitely worth the effort! For quicker preparation, substitute egg roll wrappers or prepared yeasted dough for the homemade dough.

CALLS FOR:
Ground seitan

SUGGESTED
PREPARATION METHOD:
Baking

YIELD:
8 piroshki

FILLING
2 cups ground seitan (about 1 pound)
1 cup diced onion
1 recipe Savory Seasoning Blend (page 21)
1 tablespoon parsley flakes
2 teaspoons paprika
1 teaspoon oregano

DOUGH
1 cup whole wheat pastry flour
1 cup unbleached white flour
1 teaspoon baking powder
½ teaspoon celery seeds
¼ teaspoon sea salt
6 tablespoons corn oil
½ cup plus 1 tablespoon water

GLAZE
¼ cup plain soymilk or Rice Dream beverage
½ teaspoon natural soy sauce

1. Combine all the filling ingredients in a large bowl and refrigerate for at least 30 minutes, or chill in the freezer for 10 minutes.
2. While the filling chills, prepare the dough. Combine the flours, baking powder, celery seeds, and salt in a large bowl. Pour the oil into the center of these dry ingredients, and combine with a fork or pastry blender until the mixture resembles pea-size balls. Add the water and mix quickly but gently to form a semisoft, flexible dough. Cover with wax paper to keep moist.

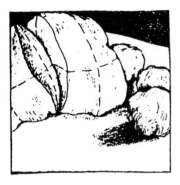

Step 1
*Form the dough
into balls.*

Step 2
*Place a ball between
layers of wax paper
and flatten it with
the palm of your hand.*

3. Preheat the oven to 350°F. Cut four 16-inch pieces of wax paper, fold each piece in half (like a book), and set them aside. (Each piece of wax paper will be used twice to roll out the dough for the turnovers.)

4. Divide the dough into 8 equal pieces and roll the pieces into balls (see Step 1). Open up one of the folded pieces of wax paper and place a dough ball on the bottom half. Cover the dough with the top half of wax paper. With the palm of your hand, gently press the dough to a ½-inch-thick circle (see Step 2).

5. With a rolling pin, roll the dough into an ⅛-inch thickness (see Step 3). Turn the entire wax-paper package over. The piece of wax paper on top will be wrinkled, so lift it up to release the wrinkles, then lay the paper back on the dough. Continue to roll the dough until it is about 6-inches in diameter.

6. Turn the package over once again and gently lift up the top piece of wax paper. Place 3 tablespoons of the seitan filling on half of the circle, spreading it to ½ inch from the edge (see Step 4). Dip your finger in water and moisten the edge of the circle of dough.

Step 3
*Roll out the dough between layers
of wax paper.*

Step 4
Place the filling on half the dough.

Step 5
Fold the empty half of the dough over the filled half.

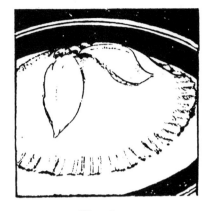

Step 6
Attach decorative pieces of dough to the piroshki.

7. Lifting the wax paper, gently fold the empty half of the dough over the filled half, forming a semicircle (see Step 5). Peel back the paper and gently press the edges of the dough together to seal. Trim away about ¼ inch of the turnover to make a smooth edge. Flute the edges or seal with the tines of a fork.

8. Repeat with the remaining dough and filling. Combine the leftover dough (from trimming the turnovers) and roll it out. Using a knife or cookie cutter, cut the dough into decorative leaves or other shapes. Moisten one side of these decorative pieces and place that side down on top of the piroshki (see Step 6). Arrange the piroshki on a lightly oiled baking sheet and place in the oven.

9. Combine the soymilk and soy sauce in a small bowl and set aside.

10. After they have baked 25 minutes, remove the piroshki from the oven and lightly brush them with the soymilk glaze. Return them to the oven for 5–8 minutes, or until they are golden brown.

11. Transfer the piping hot piroshki to a wire rack and allow to cool at least 10 minutes before serving.

SPICY SEITAN SAUSAGE

CALLS FOR:
Gluten made from
gluten flour

SUGGESTED
COOKING METHODS:
Pan-simmering,
then oven-braising

YIELD:
4 sausage links,
8–9 inches long

This versatile vegetarian-style sausage is easy to prepare. Once cooked and sliced, it can be added to soups and salads, or used as a savory pizza topping. For an unusual snack, try Pepperoni Jerky Chips (page 38).

2 cups gluten flour
1 recipe Spicy Seasoning Blend (page 21)
½ cup canola oil or sesame oil
1 cup water
1 recipe Basic Broth (page 20), less ginger ingredient
4 teaspoons canola oil or sesame oil

1. Preheat the oven to 400°F.
2. In a large bowl, combine the gluten flour and Spicy Seasoning Blend. Drizzle ½ cup of oil over the surface of the seasoned flour and mix well with a fork. Slowly pour the water over this mixture while stirring rapidly until the gluten dough is moist. Knead well to blend the seasonings.
3. Divide the gluten into 4 pieces, rolling each piece into an 8- to 9-inch-long "rope."
4. Flatten, then roll each "rope" into a long cylinder. To maintain this shape during the cooking stage, wrap cotton string in a spiral fashion around each cylinder (see illustration).
5. In a heavy, flame- and ovenproof casserole* with a lid, heat the Basic Broth on the stovetop until the broth begins to boil. Reduce the heat to low, add the gluten, and simmer 20–30 minutes.
6. Transfer the casserole dish to the oven for 20 minutes. Reduce the heat to 275°F, and continue to oven-braise the gluten, turning the links every 20 minutes until most of the broth has been absorbed (45–60 minutes). When you have turned the links for the last time, drizzle 1 teaspoon of oil over each.
7. Uncover and bake the sausages, turning them every 5 minutes for even browning. Very little broth should remain.

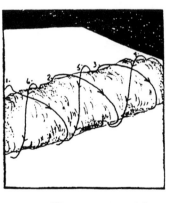

Wrap a cotton string around the gluten cylinder, following arrows 1–6.

8. Remove the dish from the oven and allow the seitan to cool completely before carefully removing the string.
9. Enjoy as you would any sausage.

* The links will nearly double in size as they cook, so select a casserole dish that is large enough to accommodate the cooked pieces of seitan. If you do not have a flameproof casserole, use a saucepan for Step 5, then transfer the gluten to a casserole dish for the remaining steps.

Variation

For hickory sausage, add 2 teaspoons of liquid hickory-smoke flavoring to the Basic Broth. This natural flavoring is found in natural foods stores and most supermarkets.

CARROTS IN BLANKETS

CALLS FOR:
Gluten

SUGGESTED COOKING METHOD:
Pan-simmering

YIELD:
4–6 servings

These quickly prepared little packages make a wonderful side dish. They are also perfect as an appetizer.

1 cup gluten
3 large carrots,* cut into 2-inch pieces
(about ¾ inch in diameter)
2 cups seasoned stock
Watercress for garnish

* You can substitute parsnips or cooked burdock root for the carrots.

1. Press and stetch the gluten to a ¼-inch thickness. Cut the gluten into 1-x-2-inch strips. Carefully stretch the strips until they are very thin. Wrap each strip snugly around a piece of carrot and secure with a toothpick.
2. In a large saucepan, bring the stock to a low boil. Add the gluten packages, cover, and simmer until the carrots are tender (about 20 minutes). Turn the carrots frequently as they simmer.
3. Transfer the carrot packages to a serving plate (leaving on the toothpicks), garnish with watercress, and enjoy hot or at room temperature.

CURRIED CUBES WITH RAISINS AND ROASTED PEANUTS ON A BED OF ROMAINE

CALLS FOR:
Seitan cubes

SUGGESTED
COOKING METHOD:
Broiling,
then pan-simmering

YIELD:
6 servings

Broiled seitan cubes are coated with a raisin-sweetened curry sauce and topped with roasted peanuts.

2 cups (about 1 pound) seitan cubes (1 inch)
Toasted (dark) sesame oil to coat seitan pieces
½ head romaine lettuce, shredded
½ cup roasted peanuts

CURRY SAUCE
1½ cups water
2-inch piece kombu
½ cup raisins
3 tablespoons arrowroot or kuzu
¼ cup water
1 tablespoon curry powder
1 tablespoon mirin
1 tablespoon natural soy sauce

1. Place seitan cubes on a baking sheet and use a pastry brush to coat them lightly with the sesame oil. Broil the cubes until they are crispy on all sides (about 8 minutes). Set aside.
2. While the seitan is broiling, prepare the sauce. In a medium saucepan, combine 1½ cups water with the kombu, bring it to a boil, then reduce the heat to low. Simmer the kombu for 2 minutes, then remove it from the pan. Add the raisins.
3. In a cup or small bowl, dissolve the arrowroot and curry powder in ¼ cup of water. Add this mixture along with the mirin and soy sauce to the raisin stock. Continue to stir until the sauce becomes thick and glossy (2–5 minutes). Add the seitan cubes and heat thoroughly. (Be careful not to overcook the sauce or it will become watery.)

4. On a large platter, arrange the lettuce leaves and top with the hot seitan cubes. Garnish with the roasted peanuts and serve immediately.

CUTLETS IN PEANUT SAUCE

Steamed greens and brown basmati rice are the perfect companions to this peppery, easy-to-prepare dish.

CALLS FOR:
Seitan cutlets

SUGGESTED
COOKING METHOD:
Pan-simmering

YIELD:
6 cutlets
(½ inch thick)

6 seitan cutlets (about 2 pounds)
1 cup water
1 recipe Aromatic Seasoning Blend (page 21)
2 tablespoons mirin
2 tablespoons natural peanut butter
2 tablespoons sweet white miso
¼ teaspoon Chinese hot pepper oil
2 scallions, chopped fine

1. In a large heavy skillet, add half the water, the Aromatic Seasoning Blend, and mirin, and heat over medium heat. Add the seitan, cover, and simmer 5–10 minutes.
2. While the seitan is simmering, combine the peanut butter, miso, remaining water, and pepper oil in a small bowl. Mix the ingredients well to form a creamy paste.
3. Transfer the cutlets temporarily to a platter, then add the peanut butter mixture to the skillet and combine it well with the broth. Return the cutlets to the skillet, cover, and simmer for 10 minutes on each side.
4. Remove the cover from the skillet, add the scallions, and simmer the cutlets, uncovered, until most of the liquid has evaporated.
5. Transfer the hot cutlets to a platter and serve with basmati rice.

MARJORIE SARMIENTO'S BRAISED SEITAN IN WINE SAUCE WITH ARTICHOKE HEARTS

CALLS FOR:
Seitan cutlets

SUGGESTED
COOKING METHOD:
Pan-simmering

YIELD:
6 servings

In this dish, seitan cutlets, marinated artichoke hearts, broccoli, and red bell peppers are simmered in a flavorful white wine sauce.

8 seitan cutlets (about 2 pounds)
1 jar (14 ounces) marinated artichoke hearts
½ cup corn flour
1 recipe Aromatic Seasoning Blend (page 21),
or ¼ teaspoon black pepper and
½ teaspoon ground coriander
1 tablespoon olive oil
3 bell peppers (red, yellow, and/or orange), seeded and cut
into eighths
¼ cup white wine
4 cups broccoli flowerets (2 inches), blanched

1. Reserving the marinade, drain the artichoke hearts and set aside.
2. In a large bowl, combine the corn flour with the Aromatic Seasoning Blend. Coat the seitan cutlets with this seasoned flour.
3. Heat the oil in a large heavy skillet over high heat. Add the coated seitan and brown on both sides. Add the bell peppers, wine, and 3 tablespoons of the reserved artichoke marinade. Cover tightly, reduce the heat to medium, and cook for 5–10 minutes.
4. Mix in the broccoli, drained artichoke hearts, and 2 tablespoons of the artichoke marinade. Continue to cook the ingredients, loosely covered, until thoroughly heated (3–5 minutes).
5. Serve hot with basmati rice.

ROASTED SEITAN WITH RED-YELLOW-ORANGE PEPPERS AND PORTOBELLO MUSHROOMS

CALLS FOR:
Seitan cutlets

SUGGESTED COOKING METHOD:
Baking

YIELD:
6 servings

This earthy, fragrant dish is best served just out of the oven, when its colors and aromas are at their peak.

6 seitan cutlets (about 1½ pounds),
cut into 12 half-inch-thick squares
3 large bell peppers (red, yellow, and/or orange),
seeded and cut into sixths
2 medium zucchini (about 7 inches long)
2 Portobello mushrooms
Olive oil for coating seitan and vegetables
¼ teaspoon sea salt
Black pepper to taste

1. Preheat the oven to 450°F. Lightly oil a 2- to 4-inch-deep baking dish (no larger than 9 x 13 inches) and set aside.
2. Blot the seitan with paper towel to remove surface moisture. Slice the zucchini lengthwise into quarters, then cut each quarter in half crosswise. Trim the rough end from the mushroom stems, then remove each stem about 1 inch from the cap. Cut the caps into sixths and the stems into long slender pieces.
3. Arrange the seitan and vegetables in the baking dish, and lightly and evenly coat them with olive oil. Sprinkle with salt and top with black pepper.
4. Place the uncovered dish in the oven and immediately reduce the temperature to 400°F. Bake the seitan and vegetables for 15 minutes, then stir the vegetables and turn the seitan pieces. Bake another 15 minutes.
5. Serve this hot dish with pasta or polenta and a green salad.

ZUCCHINI, PEPPERS, AND PORTOBELLO MUSHROOMS BAKED WITH SEITAN AND DILL IN PARCHMENT

CALLS FOR:
Seitan cutlets

SUGGESTED COOKING METHOD:
Baking

YIELD:
6 servings

Baking seitan and vegetables in parchment paper is a wonderful way to retain flavors and juices without using oil. Parchment baking paper, which comes in either in precut sheets or rolls (like wax paper), is sold in cooking supply stores.

6 seitan cutlets (about 1½ pounds), cut in half
2 medium zucchini (about 7 inches long)
2 medium bell peppers (red, orange, and/or yellow),
seeded and cut into sixths
2 Portobello mushrooms
⅛ teaspoon sea salt
1 teaspoon dill
6 sheets parchment baking paper
(approximately 12 x 16 inches)

1. Preheat the oven to 400°F.
2. Cut the zucchini crosswise into 2-inch pieces. Stand the pieces on end and cut each into ¼-inch-thick slices. Trim the rough end from the mushroom stems, then remove each stem about 1 inch from the cap. Cut the caps into sixths and the stems into long slender pieces.
3. Lay out the pieces of parchment. On each piece (slightly to one side of center), place 2 pieces each of the seitan, zucchini, peppers, and mushrooms. Sprinkle each packet with sea salt and dill.
4. To close each packet, fold the empty half of the parchment over the side with the filling. Fold and twist the edges to seal the packet. Complete the seal by twisting the last corner piece and tucking it under the parchment package, which will be an elongated semicircle.
5. Arrange the packets on a baking sheet, place in the oven, and reduce the temperature to 375°F. Bake for about 20 minutes.

6. Serve the sealed hot packets straight from the oven. Once opened, the cooking juices can be used to flavor accompanying servings of rice, millet, or pasta.

8
ELEGANT ENTRÉES AND HEARTY CASSEROLES

The discovery of a new dish does more for human
happiness than the discovery of a new star.

—Brillat-Savarin (1755–1826)
Physiologie du Gout

One of the most enjoyable aspects of cooking with seitan is experiencing the variety of dishes that can be made from this remarkable food. The recipes in this chapter range from elaborate entrées such as fragrant Coriander-Braised Seitan (page 136), to hearty, wholesome one-dish meals like Fennie's Dutch Casserole (page 144). Elegant Seitan Rolls Braised in Sake Sauce (page 142), creamy Seitan Stroganoff (page 139), and festive Tricolor Pilaf (page 145) are just a sampling of the assortment of recipes presented in this chapter.

CORIANDER-BRAISED SEITAN

CALLS FOR:
Seitan

**SUGGESTED
COOKING METHOD:**
Pan-simmering

YIELD:
4–6 servings

You can prepare this dish in just minutes. The aroma of the seitan simmering in a coriander sauce will draw your hungry diners to the kitchen.

4 cups seitan (about 2 pounds)
1 tablespoon sesame oil
1 tablespoon toasted (dark) sesame oil
1 tablespoon minced fresh garlic
1 tablespoon minced fresh ginger
3 tablespoons molasses
3 tablespoons natural soy sauce
3 tablespoons ground coriander
1 teaspoon black pepper
⅛ teaspoon hot pepper oil
½ cup rice wine
3 scallions, cut into 2-inch lengths

1. Using forks, pull apart the seitan into irregular shapes.
2. In a heavy skillet with a cover, heat the two types of sesame oil together over medium heat. Add the garlic and ginger, and sauté until the garlic begins to brown (2–5 minutes).
3. Add the seitan pieces to the skillet and sauté over medium heat until browned and a little crispy (about 15 minutes).
4. While the seitan is browning, combine the molasses, soy sauce, coriander, black pepper, and hot pepper oil in a small bowl. Add this mixture to the skillet, coating the seitan evenly. Add the rice wine. Cover and simmer for 5 minutes.
5. Uncover the skillet, add the scallions, and increase the heat to high. Continue to simmer the seitan for about 1 minute, or until the liquid has been reduced to a coating for the seitan.
6. Serve over couscous or brown rice as a main or side dish. As an appetizer, serve Coriander-Braised Seitan with chilled radishes and cucumbers.

CREAMY FETTUCCINE WITH CRISPY SEITAN STRIPS

CALLS FOR:
Seitan cutlets

SUGGESTED
COOKING METHOD:
Broiling

YIELD:
4 servings

Green fettuccine and crispy strips of seitan are coated with a creamy basil-garlic sauce.

4 seitan cutlets (about 1 pound) cut into strips
(2 x ¼ inches)
1 pound green (spinach) fettuccine
1 teaspoon kuzu
1⅓ cups water
1 tablespoon tahini
1 teaspoon natural soy sauce
¼ teaspoon sea salt
½ teaspoon dried basil
1 clove garlic, crushed and minced
¾ cup plain soymilk or Rice Dream beverage
Minced fresh parsley for garnish

1. Place the seitan strips on a lightly oiled baking sheet and broil until crispy (about 3 minutes on each side). Set aside.
2. Cook the fettuccine al dente, then drain and rinse thoroughly under cold water.
3. Dissolve the kuzu in the water. Add the tahini and mix with a fork until smooth. Add the soy sauce, salt, basil, garlic, and soymilk. Combine well.
4. Heat a heavy skillet over medium heat, and brush it lightly with oil. Add the cooked noodles and heat them thoroughly, turning them frequently to prevent burning.
5. Add the seasoned kuzu-tahini mixture to the noodles. Mix together gently. Lower the heat when bubbles appear. The sauce should look milky. Cover the pan, reduce the heat, and simmer for 10 minutes.
6. Remove the cover and mix the noodles carefully as the sauce thickens. Allow the sauce to simmer until it is the desired consistency. If the sauce is too thick, thin it with some water (a little at a time, and no more than ½ cup). Adjust the seasonings.

7. Just before serving, add the seitan strips to the noodles and mix together gently. Garnish with a few seitan strips and minced parsley.

BURGERS DIABLO

CALLS FOR:
Ground seitan

SUGGESTED
COOKING METHOD:
Pan-frying

YIELD:
4 quarter-pound
burgers

Top these tasty burgers with barbecue sauce, mustard, or the condiment of your choice. They are easy to prepare and take only twenty-five minutes to cook.

2 cups ground seitan (about 1 pound)
6 tablespoons chickpea flour
3–6 tablespoons whole wheat pastry flour
1 tablespoon parsley flakes
1 tablespoon paprika
½ teaspoon garlic granules
½ teaspoon black pepper
¼ teaspoon sea salt
Sesame oil for pan-frying burgers
2–4 teaspoons natural soy sauce (½–1 teaspoon per burger)

1. In a large bowl, combine all the ingredients except the sesame oil and soy sauce. Form this mixture into four ½-inch-thick patties, about 4 inches in diameter.
2. In a heavy skillet, heat the oil and pan-fry the burgers over medium heat (8–10 minutes per side). Keep the heat high enough to cook the burgers thoroughly, yet low enough to prevent them from burning.
3. Before turning the burgers, sprinkle each with a little soy sauce and spread it evenly over the tops. Turn the burgers over, then gently flatten them a little with a spatula. When the second side is cooked, top with more soy sauce and turn the burgers over to the first side to continue browning for about 5 seconds.
4. Serve as an open-faced sandwich or in a bun, accompanied by your favorite condiments and garnishes.

SEITAN STROGANOFF

CALLS FOR:
Seitan strips

SUGGESTED
COOKING METHOD:
Pan-simmering

YIELD:
6 servings

For a family-style meal or an elegant buffet, serve this creamy, mushroom-filled stew with wild rice or broad noodles. Accompanied by a crisp salad or steamed greens, it is an especially satisfying meal.

2 cups (about 1 pound) seitan strips (2 x ¼ inches)
1 tablespoon sesame oil
2 cups diced onions
1 pound mushrooms, quartered or cut into ¼-inch slices
2 teaspoons sea salt
½ teaspoon white pepper
3–3½ cups water
1 pound tofu
1 tablespoon umeboshi paste
3 tablespoons thick starch (from making homemade gluten)*
½ cup sake or dry white wine
¼ cup minced parsley for garnish

* Can use 3 tablespoons of arrowroot or kuzu dissolved in ¾ cup water, in place of the thick starch.

1. In a large heavy saucepan, heat the oil and lightly brown the onions. Add the mushrooms, salt, and pepper, and sauté 8–10 minutes. Add the seitan strips and water, and simmer for 15 minutes.
2. While the seitan and vegetables are simmering, purée the tofu, umeboshi paste, and starch together in a blender until smooth.
3. Ten minutes before serving, add the wine and tofu mixture to the simmering seitan. Heat this sauce thoroughly while mixing, until it is thick and smooth. Adjust the seasonings. Be careful not to overheat the sauce, or it will separate and lose its creamy consistency.
4. Top the stroganoff with parsley and serve immediately over brown rice or broad noodles.

SEITAN PEPPERONI CASSEROLE "DIJON" WITH POTATOES AND OLIVES

CALLS FOR:
Seitan sausage

SUGGESTED
COOKING METHOD:
Baking

YIELD:
6 servings

The pepperoni-like flavor of Spicy Seitan Sausage combines well with mustard and potatoes in this unusual casserole.

1 or 2 links Spicy Seitan Sausage (page 126),
cut into ¼-inch rounds
8 medium unpeeled potatoes, scrubbed
½ cup plain soymilk or Rice Dream beverage
2 tablespoons Dijon-style mustard
½–¾ teaspoon sea salt
¼–½ cup cornmeal
2 tablespoons corn oil
2 teaspoons natural soy sauce
10–12 black olives
1 teaspoon paprika

1. Boil the potatoes in a large pot of water until they are tender. Drain and place in a bowl. Mash the potatoes and mix in the soymilk, mustard, and salt.
2. Preheat the oven to 375°F. Generously oil a 9-x-9-x-2-inch baking dish with a cover, and dust the inside with the cornmeal.
3. Arrange half the seitan slices on top of the cornmeal. Evenly spread the potatoes on top. Push the remaining seitan slices into the potatoes until they are half buried.
4. Mix the corn oil and soy sauce together, then drizzle it over the top of the casserole.* Arrange the olives on top and sprinkle with paprika. Cover and bake for 45 minutes, then remove the cover and bake 5–10 minutes more to brown the top slightly.
5. Serve hot.

* If the potatoes touch the cover of the baking dish, be sure to oil the inside cover. This will prevent the potatoes from sticking to the cover while the casserole bakes.

CUTLETS BROILED IN MUSHROOM SAUCE

Whether you use the Aromatic Seasoning Blend or seasonings of your choice, the texture and flavor of these pan-fried cutlets provide a tempting main dish.

CALLS FOR:
Seitan cutlets

SUGGESTED
COOKING METHOD:
Pan-frying,
then broiling

YIELD:
6 servings

6–8 thin seitan cutlets (1½–2 pounds), chilled
Combination of ½ cup chickpea flour, ½ cup corn flour,
and 1 tablespoon arrowroot flour (or 1 cup corn flour
plus 1 tablespoon unbleached white flour)
3–4 tablespoons sesame oil for frying cutlets

MUSHROOM SAUCE
2 teaspoons sesame oil
10–12 mushrooms, sliced very thin
1½ cups water
3 tablespoons natural soy sauce
1 tablespoon mirin
1½ tablespoons lemon juice
1 recipe Aromatic Seasoning Blend (page 21), optional
¾ cup plain soymilk or Rice Dream beverage

1. Combine the flours in a pie plate or other shallow dish. Press both sides of each cutlet into the flour and coat well.
2. In a heavy skillet, heat 1–2 tablespoons of the sesame oil and pan-fry the cutlets until they are golden brown. Add more oil to the pan as needed. Remove the cooked cutlets from the pan and set aside.
3. To make the sauce, add the mushrooms and a little oil (no more than 2 teaspoons) to the skillet, and sauté the mushrooms briefly over medium-low heat. Add the water, soy sauce, mirin, lemon juice, and Aromatic Seasoning Blend (if using). Simmer the mushrooms until they are tender (3–5 minutes).
4. Stir the soymilk into the remaining flour mixture to make a smooth paste. Add this paste to the skillet and slowly

stir until the sauce has thickened slightly. (This gravy should be light, not too thick.) Adjust the seasonings.

5. Lightly oil a 3-inch deep, ovenproof serving dish. Arrange the cutlets in the dish and cover with the mushroom sauce. Broil for 3 minutes.

6. Serve this dish immediately, accompanied by your favorite steamed greens.

SEITAN ROLLS
BRAISED IN SAKE SAUCE

CALLS FOR:
Gluten

SUGGESTED
COOKING METHODS:
Steaming,
then oven-braising

YIELD:
4 servings

Seasoned rice and leeks are wrapped in gluten, then steamed and oven-braised in a flavorful sake sauce. This dish is a real adventure in cooking with seitan!

2 cups gluten
2 teaspoons Dijon-style mustard
¼ cup sesame oil
1 onion, quartered
2 carrots, cut into 1-inch chunks
1 tablespoon arrowroot

FILLING
2 tablespoons olive oil
4 medium leeks, cleaned and chopped fine
2 cups sticky cooked rice
1 teaspoon dried thyme
1 teaspoon sea salt
2 large cloves garlic, crushed and minced

SAKE STOCK
1 cup water
1 recipe Hearty Seasoning Blend (page 21)
1 cup sake

1. To make the filling for the rolls, first heat the olive oil in a heavy skillet. Add the leeks and sauté them until they are bright green. Transfer the leeks to a bowl and combine

them with the rice, thyme, salt, garlic, and allspice. Set aside.

2. Divide the gluten into four equal pieces. Take one piece and stretch it carefully into an 8-x-10-inch rectangle (the 8-inch side should be closest to you).

3. Spread ½ teaspoon of mustard over the surface of the gluten. Place ¼ of the rice mixture on the third of the rectangle that is closest to you. Spread the mixture to an even thickness, but leave 2 inches on the right and left sides empty, as well as 1 inch on the front edge.

4. Bring the front edge of the gluten (the edge closest to you) up and fold it over the filling, then fold in the right and left sides of the gluten to enclose the filling. Gently roll up the package. Any protruding or bulky side edges should be stretched across to the opposite side of the roll for a uniform thickness.

5. Tie the filled roll with enough string to secure it on all sides, then set it aside. Repeat with the remaining gluten and filling.

6. Line a vegetable steamer with a clean damp cloth and place it in a pot with 1–2 inches of water (see Figure 8.1). Bring the water to boil. Steam the rolls for 5–10 minutes, then carefully transfer them to a plate to cool. (The rolls are very fragile when hot but will become more firm as they cool.)

7. While the rolls cool, preheat the oven to 400°F. Heat the Sake Stock ingredients in a small saucepan.

8. In a flameproof baking dish, heat the sesame oil over medium heat. Brown the steamed, filled seitan rolls in this dish until they are crispy on all sides. Add the onion and carrot pieces to the browned rolls.

9. Top the rolls with the hot stock, cover, and braise in the oven for 10 minutes. Reduce the oven heat to 300°F and continue to braise for 1 hour, basting the rolls occasionally. After an hour, dissolve the arrowroot in a tablespoon of sake and add it the remaining broth. Stir until a thick sauce forms.

10. Remove the strings from the rolls. Top the rolls with sauce and serve.

Figure 8.1
Lined vegetable steamer.

FENNIE'S DUTCH CASSEROLE

CALLS FOR:
Seitan cutlets

SUGGESTED
COOKING METHOD:
Baking

YIELD:
5 servings

Warm up on a cold day with a hearty combination of seitan, mashed potatoes, and sauerkraut. This delicious, Old World-style casserole is quick and easy to prepare.

6–8 seitan cutlets (1½–2 pounds)
4–5 medium to large unpeeled potatoes
½ cup plain soymilk or Rice Dream beverage
1 teaspoon sea salt
3 cups sauerkraut, drained and squeezed
1 teaspoon corn oil
1 teaspoon natural soy sauce

1. Boil the potatoes in a large pot of water until they are tender. Drain and place in a bowl. Mash the potatoes, mixing in the soymilk and salt.
2. Preheat the oven to 400°F. Oil a deep 2½- or 3-quart casserole dish that has a cover.
3. Put two-thirds of the mashed potatoes in the bottom of the baking dish and pack it to an even thickness. Top with the sauerkraut, pressing it lightly into the potatoes.
4. If the cutlets are more than ½ inch thick, slice them in half, then arrange them on top of the sauerkraut, setting aside a few pieces for the top of the casserole. Next, add a layer of the remaining mashed potatoes. Slice the remaining seitan into strips and arrange them on top of the potatoes.
5. Mix the corn oil and soy sauce together, then drizzle it over the top of the casserole. Cover and bake for 30 minutes, then remove the cover and bake the casserole 10 minutes more to brown the top.*
6. Serve hot, accompanied by a soup of puréed, sweet winter squash and a crisp salad.

* If the potatoes touch the cover of the baking dish, be sure to oil the inside cover. This will prevent the potatoes from sticking to the cover as the casserole bakes.

TRICOLOR PILAF

This colorful pilaf has the addition of uniquely textured deep-fried bits of gluten.

CALLS FOR:
Gluten

SUGGESTED
COOKING METHOD:
Deep-frying

YIELD:
4–6 servings

1 cup gluten
1½ cups uncooked long-grain brown rice
3¼–3½ cups water
1 teaspoon sesame oil or olive oil
1 cup diced carrots
¼ teaspoon sea salt
2 teaspoons natural soy sauce
Oil for deep-frying
1 cup fresh or frozen corn kernels
1 cup freshly shelled or frozen green peas

1. Rinse the rice in a strainer and set it aside to drain. In a saucepan, bring the water to a boil.
2. In a heavy pot, heat the sesame oil over medium heat. Add the carrots, and sauté them for about 5 minutes. Add the rice and continue to sauté, stirring constantly until the rice is a light golden-brown color and fairly dry. Very slowly, add the boiling water. Then add the sea salt and soy sauce. Cover the pot and bring the ingredients to a boil over high heat.
3. Reduce the heat to low and place a flame diffuser under the pot. Simmer the rice until it is light and fluffy (50–60 minutes).
4. While the rice is simmering, heat 2–3 inches of oil in a 3- or 4-quart saucepan. Break off tiny pieces of the gluten and carefully drop them into the oil. Briefly deep-fry until they are golden brown. Place the cooked pieces on paper towels to remove any excess oil.
5. In a separate saucepan, steam the corn and peas until tender.
6. When the rice is done, add the corn, peas, and seitan, and mix together gently. Serve immediately.

Variation

Feel free to use a variety of cooked or raw vegetables in this pilaf such as diced celery, green and red bell peppers, broccoli, or cubed winter squash. You might also add minced fresh parsley or other fresh herbs.

PAN-SIMMERED CUTLETS WITH ONIONS

CALLS FOR:
Seitan cutlets

SUGGESTED COOKING METHOD:
Pan-simmering

YIELD:
6 servings

These hearty, old-fashioned pan-simmered cutlets are quick to prepare. Mashed potatoes and a green salad complete the meal. Try serving this dish with a flavorful chutney, cranberry sauce, or applesauce.

12 seitan cutlets (about 3 pounds)
¼ cup sesame oil
2 medium onions, sliced crosswise into ¼-inch rounds
and separated into rings
2 tablespoons minced parsley

1. Heat the oil in a large heavy skillet with a cover over medium-high heat. Add the cutlets and brown them on both sides.
2. Top the browned cutlets with the onions, cover the skillet, and reduce the heat to low. Cook the ingredients until the onions are soft (about 10 minutes). Carefully turn over the seitan and onions, cover again, and continue to cook until the onions are translucent and lightly browned (about 8 minutes). Stir the seitan and onions occasionally to prevent them from burning.
3. Transfer the cooked onions to a serving platter, top with the cutlets, and garnish with parsley.

PASTICHIO— GREEK-STYLE MACARONI CASSEROLE

CALLS FOR:
Ground seitan

SUGGESTED COOKING METHODS:
Pan-browning, then baking

YIELD:
6 servings

This version of pastichio calls for ground seitan and a light creamy sauce that is flavored with a hint of cinnamon. The pasta used in this golden-crusted adaptation of a traditional Greek dish resembles very long tubes of elbow macaroni. Made specifically for pastichio, this pasta can be found in Greek markets, as well as the imported foods section of some supermarkets. (Fettuccine or other broad flat pasta can be substituted for the traditional pastichio pasta.)

2 cups coarsely ground seitan (about 1 pound)
16 ounces pastichio pasta or a broad flat pasta
3 tablespoons olive oil or sesame oil
1½ tablespoons natural soy sauce
1 cup bread crumbs

SAUCE
1½ tablespoons kuzu or arrowroot
1–1½ cups water
1½ cups plain soymilk or Rice Dream beverage
1 tablespoon tahini
¾ teaspoon sea salt
½ teaspoon cinnamon

1. Preheat the oven to 400°F. Lightly oil a 9-x-13-inch baking dish and set aside.
2. While the oven is preheating, cook the pasta until al dente, then drain and place in a bowl.
3. In a large skillet, heat the oil, then add the seitan. Brown the seitan for 3–4 minutes, then add the soy sauce. Combine the browned seitan with the drained pasta, mix it together, and set aside.
4. To prepare the sauce, dissolve the kuzu in ½ cup of the water and set it aside. In a saucepan, heat the soymilk, another ½ cup of water, the tahini, salt, and cinnamon over medium heat, stirring constantly until the mixture

is almost boiling. Add the dissolved kuzu to the pot and stir this sauce as it thickens. If the sauce gets too thick, add a little more water (no more than ½ cup). Adjust the seasonings.

5. To assemble the casserole, first layer half the pasta-seitan combination in the bottom of the prepared baking dish. Pour half the sauce evenly over the top, add the rest of the pasta, and cover with the remaining sauce. Top with a layer of bread crumbs.

6. Cover the casserole with foil and bake 15 minutes. Remove the foil and bake another 15 minutes to brown the crust.

7. Serve hot.

POLENTA MARINARA WITH SAVORY GROUND SEITAN

CALLS FOR:
Ground seitan

SUGGESTED
COOKING METHOD:
Baking

YIELD:
6 servings

Bright golden-colored polenta is topped with seasoned ground seitan and your favorite marinara sauce in this entrée, which takes less than an hour to bake. If you prepare this dish in advance, keep the sauce and polenta separate until ready to bake.

2 cups coarsely ground seitan
2½ teaspoons black pepper
2 teaspoons sage
1½ teaspoons garlic granules
1 teaspoon paprika
½ teaspoon nutmeg
½ teaspoon dry mustard
1 medium onion, chopped very fine
1½ cups prepared marinara sauce

POLENTA
1½ cups cornmeal
½ teaspoon sea salt
4–6 cups water

1. To prepare the polenta, combine the cornmeal, salt, and 4 cups of the water in a heavy saucepan and heat over medium heat. Stir constantly as the cornmeal begins to thicken. When the cornmeal starts to boil, add the remaining 2 cups of water while stirring briskly.
2. Reduce the heat to low and place a flame diffuser under the pot. Cover and simmer the mixture for about 40 minutes, stirring and checking the consistency every 10 minutes. It should be smooth and thick but not stiff.
3. Evenly spread the cooked polenta in a lightly oiled 10-inch square baking dish. Allow the polenta to cool at room temperature for at least 30 minutes.
4. When the polenta is firm, preheat the oven to 375°F.
5. In a medium bowl, combine the seitan, black pepper, sage, garlic granules, paprika, nutmeg, mustard and onion. Mix together well.

6. Spread the marinara sauce evenly over the polenta. Top with the seasoned seitan-onion mixture. Cover with foil and bake for 30 minutes. Remove the foil and continue to bake for 15 minutes. Longer baking time may be needed if the polenta has been refrigerated prior to baking.
7. Serve hot.

SUMMERTOWN PATTIES

CALLS FOR:
Gluten made from
gluten flour

SUGGESTED
COOKING METHOD:
Baking

YIELD:
10–15 seitan patties

Created by the folks at The Farm in Summertown, Tennessee, this recipe begins with a quick, easy way to make your own gluten from scratch. The gluten is seasoned, formed into patties, then baked. Feel free to add your choice of seasonings.

4 cups gluten flour
½–1 teaspoon garlic granules
½ cup brown rice or barley miso
3 cups water

1. Preheat the oven to 350°F. Lightly oil a baking sheet and set aside.
2. In a large bowl, combine the gluten flour and garlic and set aside.
3. Place the miso in a medium bowl. Add the water a little at a time, mixing it with the miso until smooth.
4. Add the miso to the seasoned gluten flour, stirring it vigorously with a fork until it develops a uniform, elastic consistency. Knead the gluten and form it into a loaf.
5. Tear off chunks of gluten from the loaf and shape them into patties that are approximately 4 inches in diameter and ½ inch thick.
6. Arrange the patties on the baking sheet and bake them for 10–15 minutes on each side, or until they are nicely browned.
7. These patties can be eaten as is or embellished with a sauce. They can also be ground and used in other recipes.

SEITAN KEBABS

CALLS FOR:
Seitan cubes

SUGGESTED
COOKING METHOD:
Broiling

YIELD:
4–6 servings

Choose your favorite vegetables to marinate and broil with seitan cubes in these quick and easy kebabs. Feel free to use a different barbecue sauce from the one given below. Soaking wooden skewers in water for one hour before using will prevent them from burning.

2–3 cups (1–1½ pounds) seitan cubes (1–2 inches)
Assorted vegetables of choice
(good choices include whole mushrooms,
red and green bell pepper chunks, cherry tomatoes,
zucchini rounds, and pearl onions)

KEBAB SAUCE
¼ cup barley miso or brown rice miso
¼ cup tomato paste
2 garlic cloves, crushed and minced well
¼ cup grated onion
¼ cup cider vinegar
¼ cup barley malt syrup, brown rice syrup,
honey, or molasses
2 tablespoons olive oil
¼ teaspoon dry mustard
¼ teaspoon allspice

1. Prepare the sauce by combining the ingredients in a medium bowl. Add the seitan cubes and let them marinate in the sauce for 30–60 minutes.
2. Assemble the seitan and vegetables on the skewers (allow about 4 seitan cubes and 3 vegetables per skewer). Brush the vegetables with barbecue sauce and let them marinate about 15 minutes before cooking.
3. Lay the kebabs across a baking pan to catch any drips, and broil them about 6 inches from the heat source for about 8 minutes. Turn them over, baste, and broil another 4–5 minutes.
4. Serve hot.

COUNTRY POT PIES

CALLS FOR:
Seitan cubes

SUGGESTED
COOKING METHOD:
Pan-simmering,
then baking

YIELD:
8 pot pies
(4 ½ inches
in diameter)

These individual pies are ideal for lunches, buffets, or picnics. The seitan and vegetable filling may be prepared in advance and refrigerated up to twelve hours.

FILLING
3 cups (about 1½ pounds) seitan cubes (½–1 inch)
3 tablespoons sesame oil or olive oil
2 cups diced onions
2 cups diced carrots
3 celery stalks, diced
1½–2 cups water
1 bay leaf
½ teaspoon thyme
½ teaspon black pepper, or to taste
5 tablespoons thick starch
(from preparing homemade gluten)*
1 tablespoon mirin
¼ cup natural soy sauce
2 cups fresh shelled or frozen green peas
1 cup fresh or frozen corn kernels

PASTRY DOUGH
2 cups whole wheat pastry flour
2 cups unbleached white flour
½ teaspoon sea salt
2 teaspoons baking powder
¾ cup corn oil
¾–1 cup water

GLAZE
2 tablespoons corn oil
2 tablespoons natural soy sauce

* Can use 3 tablespons arrowroot or kuzu dissolved in ¼ cup water, in place of the thick starch.

1. Prepare the filling. In a 4-quart saucepan, heat the oil and sauté the onions, carrots, and celery until the onions are translucent. Add the seitan cubes and sauté 5 minutes more.

2. Add the water, bay leaf, thyme, and black pepper, and bring to a boil. Reduce the heat to medium and add the starch, stirring constantly as the sauce thickens. Add the mirin and soy sauce, and remove the pan from the heat. Stir in the peas and corn.

3. Preheat the oven to 375°F. Cut a few sheets of wax paper 12–14 inches long and set them aside. These will be used for rolling out the pastry dough.

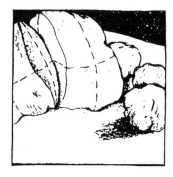

Step 1
Divide the dough evenly and form it into balls.

To Make the Dough and Assemble the Pies:

1. Combine the flours, salt, and baking powder in a medium bowl. Using a fork, blend these dry ingredients well. Add the oil all at once, mixing it with the flour to form pea-size balls. Add ¾ cup of water. Use the fork to mix it into the flour with a circular, bottom-to-top lifting motion. If the dough seems too dry, add more water 1 tablespoon at a time (no more that ¼ cup). The dough should be soft and elastic but not sticky or wet. Mix the dough gently. All the flour will pull away from the sides of the bowl as the dough forms a ball. Cover the dough and set aside for 3–5 minutes.

2. Divide the dough in half. Cut each half into 8 equal pieces (for a total of 16 pieces). Roll the pieces into balls the size of golf balls (see Step 1). Cover with a clean, damp towel.

3. Take one of the sheets of wax paper and fold it in half. Open it like a book and place one of the dough balls in the center of one side. Fold the other wax paper half on top of the dough, and flatten the dough with the palm of your hand (see Step 2). Turn the dough over and flatten it some more. Return the paper to side one.

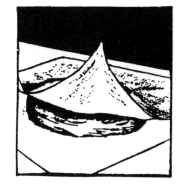

Step 2
Flatten the dough between layers of wax paper.

4. Using a rolling pin, roll out the dough from the center out to form a circle. Turn the "package" over, lift up the wax paper, and reposition it to release any wrinkles, then roll out the dough some more. Turn the package back to side one, release any wrinkles in the

wax paper, and finish rolling out the dough to a 6-inch circle (see Step 3).

5. Open the wax paper and lay the dough over the pie pan. Peel away the remaining wax paper and gently press the dough evenly in the pan (see Step 4). Fill the pie with ½ cup of the filling and top with a second circle of rolled-out dough.

6. Moisten the edges of the two crusts and press them together. Trim the crusts to extend ½ inch beyond the edge of the pie pan (see Step 5). To create a decorative edge, pinch, flute, or press the edges together with a fork. With a sharp knife or scissors, make 4 or 5 slashes in the top crust to allow steam to escape.

7. Use the leftover dough to cut out different shapes for decorating the top crust of each pie. Moisten the top crust where the decorative shape is to be placed, then press the shape onto the crust (see Step 6).

8. Mix together the corn oil and soy sauce to form a glaze, and lightly paint it on the top crust of each pie.

9. Put the pies on two cookie sheets and bake for 30 minutes until the crust is golden and the filling begins to bubble. Transfer the hot pies to a wire rack and let them cool 10–15 minutes before serving.

Step 3
Roll out the dough to a 6-inch circle.

Step 4
Line the pie pan with the dough and peel away the wax paper.

Step 5
Trim the edges of the dough.

Step 6
Country pot pie.

AUNT RUTH'S HOLIDAY "ROAST" WITH COUSCOUS STUFFING AND CHUNKY MUSHROOM GRAVY

CALLS FOR:
Gluten

A tasty alternative to a Thanksgiving turkey, this marinated gluten is filled with seasoned couscous, walnuts, and red bell peppers, then roasted to a crisp finish. Chunky Mushroom Gravy is the perfect companion to this unique roast.

SUGGESTED COOKING METHOD:
Baking

2 cups gluten

YIELD:
4–6 servings

MARINADE
¾ cup natural soy sauce
¾ cup sake or dry white wine
1 tablespoon grated ginger
2 cloves garlic, crushed and minced

STUFFING
1½ cups couscous
3 cups water
½ cup diced sweet red bell peppers
¼–½ cup chopped walnuts
¼ cup minced fresh parsley
½ teaspoon thyme
½ teaspoon sea salt

CHUNKY MUSHROOM GRAVY
2 pounds mushrooms, cut into thirds
3 medium onions, diced into 1-inch pieces
1 tablespoon sesame oil
Dash of wine vinegar
1 cup thick starch (from preparing homemade gluten)*
Natural soy sauce, to taste
Sea salt, to taste
¼ cup chopped fresh parsley

* Can use 2–3 tablespoons arrowroot or kuzu dissolved in ¼ cup water, in place of the thick starch.

1. In a medium bowl, combine all the marinade ingredients. Add the gluten and knead it well in the marinade. Cover and refrigerate overnight.

2. To prepare the stuffing (which can be assembled up to one day before using), begin by soaking the couscous in the water until all the water has been absorbed (1–2 hours). Using hot water for soaking will reduce this time. Combine the remaining stuffing ingredients with the soaked couscous and mix together well.

3. When you are ready to assemble the "roast," preheat the oven to 375°F. Line a 9-x-5-inch metal loaf pan with foil. Coat the foil with cooking oil and set the pan aside.

4. Remove the marinated gluten and reserve the marinade. Using a rolling pin, roll the gluten into an 18-inch square that is ¼-inch thick (see Step 1). Roll it quickly and firmly in all directions. (The gluten will tend to spring back to its original shape.) Quickly transfer the rolled gluten to the loaf pan (see Step 2). Hold one hand on top of the gluten to keep its shape, while loosely packing the stuffing into the loaf with the other hand (see Step 3).

5. Stretch one side of the gluten over the top of the filling and tuck it in the opposite side (see Step 4). Baste the surface with some of the reserved marinade, then stretch the gluten from the other side up and over the top of the filled loaf.

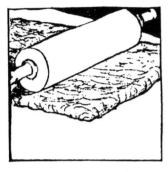

Step 1
Roll out the marinated gluten.

Step 2
Lay the flattened gluten into a foil-lined loaf pan.

Step 3
Fill the loaf with the seasoned stuffing.

Step 4
Lift and stretch the gluten, and tuck it in the opposite side.

6. Using a sharp knife, make a few small cuts in the top of the gluten. Baste the top with plenty of marinade, then place in the oven. Bake, basting every 10–15 minutes, until the top is brown and crusty and it no longer feels sticky (about 1 hour).

7. Remove the pan from the oven. After about 5 minutes, invert the loaf on a rack and remove the pan. Let the loaf cool for 20 minutes.

8. While the roast is cooling, prepare the gravy. In a medium saucepan, heat the sesame oil and sauté the mushrooms and onions until the onions are translucent. Add a dash of vinegar to bring out the flavor of the mushrooms and help them retain their color. Add enough water to cover ¾ of the mushrooms and bring to a slow boil. Add the starch and simmer for 10 minutes, stirring constantly as the sauce thickens. Season to taste with soy sauce and salt. Just before serving, stir the parsley into the sauce.

9. Carefully peel the foil from the cooled loaf and invert it right side up on a platter (see Step 5). Slice the roast and serve with Chunky Mushroom Gravy (see Step 6).

Step 5
Invert the cooked loaf, remove the pan, and peel away the foil.

Step 6
Slices of Aunt Ruth's Holiday Roast.

SAVORY MUSHROOM LASAGNE

CALLS FOR:
Seitan strips

SUGGESTED
COOKING METHODS:
Pan-simmering,
then baking

YIELD:
6–8 servings

The herbed white sauce in this layered dish adds just the right accent to the seitan and mushroom combination. Needing only forty-five minutes to bake, Savory Mushroom Lasagne is bound to be a dish you will want to prepare often.

2 cups (about 1 pound) seitan strips (2 x ½ inches)
16 ounces spinach lasagne
4 cups sliced mushrooms (about 12 ounces)
2½ tablespoons olive oil
1½ teaspoons sea salt
2 cloves garlic, crushed and minced
2 cups plain soymilk or Rice Dream beverage
1½ teaspoons water or stock
⅔ cup thick starch (from making homemade gluten)*
8 ounces soft tofu
1 tablespoon corn oil
⅔ cup dry white wine, optional
⅔ cup whole wheat bread crumbs
1 tablespoon paprika
Savory Seasoning Blend (page 21), to taste

* Can use 1 tablespoon arrowroot or kuzu dissolved in ⅔ cup water, in place of the thick starch.

1. Cook the lasagne noodles al dente. Drain.
2. While the noodles cook, preheat the oven to 400°F. Lightly oil a 9-x-13-inch baking dish and set aside.
3. In a large skillet, heat the olive oil over medium-high heat. Add the mushrooms and sauté them until tender. Reduce the heat to medium. Add the salt, garlic, and seitan, and sauté together for 2–3 minutes. Add the soymilk and water and heat until almost boiling, then stir in the thick starch. Continue to stir as the sauce thickens.
4. Crumble the tofu into the sauce and add the wine. When the sauce is thick, adjust the seasonings and remove from the heat.
5. In the prepared baking dish, alternate layers of the lasagne noodles and the sauce, ending with a top layer of sauce.

6. Combine the bread crumbs, paprika, Savory Seasoning Blend, and corn oil. Sprinkle this crumb mixture evenly over the top layer of sauce. Cover with foil.
7. Place the lasagne in the oven, reduce the temperature to 375°F, and bake for 25 minutes. Remove the foil and bake 8–10 minutes more to lightly brown the top.
8. Set the lasagne aside at room temperature for 5 minutes before serving.

9
DESERTS

Cooking is like love.
It should be entered into with abandon
or not at all.

—Harriet van Horne, 1920–

You may be surprised to discover that gluten can be used to create delicious desserts. For instance, you can roll pieces of hot deep-fried gluten in a sweet crunchy coating, as in the Cinnamon-Chestnut Puffs on page 164. To make such dessert treats as Date-Nut Filled Puffs found on page 168, simply wrap gluten around a chewy filling before baking it.

In addition, there are many delicious ways to make use of the starch water that results from making homemade gluten (see Save that Starch Water! page 23). You can use this starch to thicken puddings and sauces, or to add chewy texture to cookies.

And this is only the beginning. Use the dessert recipes from this chapter as starting points for your own unique creations.

CHEWY DATE-WALNUT COOKIES

CALLS FOR:
Thick starch

YIELD:
24–30 cookies

Use starch water from making gluten for these big, chewy malt-sweetened cookies.

2 cups walnuts
¼ teaspoon sea salt
1½ teaspoons baking powder
1 cup chopped dates*
½ cup barley malt syrup, rice syrup, or sorghum syrup
1¼ cup thick starch (from preparing homemade gluten)
½ teaspoon vanilla extract

* Before chopping the dates, sprinkle 2 tablespoons of flour (any type) on the cutting surface. The flour will coat the date pieces as they are cut and prevent them from sticking together.

1. Preheat the oven to 350°F. Lightly oil a baking sheet, or line it with wax paper or baking parchment. Set it aside.
2. Using a food processor or blender, coarsely grind the walnuts and place them in a mixing bowl, breaking up any clumps. Sprinkle the salt and baking powder over the nuts and combine thoroughly.
3. In a small bowl, blend together the syrup and thick starch until it is smooth, then stir in the vanilla. Add this mixture to the nuts and mix well.
4. Drop tablespoons of the batter about 2 inches apart on the prepared baking sheet.
5. Bake the cookies until they are golden (15–18 minutes).
6. Transfer the hot cookies to a rack and let them cool before serving.

ALMOND ESSENCE WHIP

This creamy almond-flavored pudding, which gets its rich texture from a combination of blanched almonds, kuzu, and the thick starch from making gluten, can be enjoyed plain or topped with your favorite sauce. For an unbelievable parfait, try layering Almond Essence Whip with Fudge Pudding (page 165), or fresh fruit and toasted almond slivers.

3 tablespoons thick starch (from making gluten)*
3 tablespoons kuzu
¾ cup vanilla soymilk or vanilla Rice Dream beverage
½ cup maple syrup
1 teaspoon vanilla extract
¾ teaspoon almond extract
Pinch sea salt
¼ cup water

ALMOND MIXTURE
1 cup almonds
¼ cup maple syrup
⅓ cup vanilla soymilk or vanilla Rice Dream beverage
¼–½ cup water

* For a dessert that is white in color, use thick starch that is derived from unbleached white flour. Starch from other flour combinations is usable but will result in a darker-colored pudding.

1. In a small saucepan, combine the thick starch, kuzu, and half the soymilk. Stir to dissolve the kuzu. Add the remaining soymilk along with the maple syrup, vanilla and almond extracts, salt, and water. Stir this mixture constantly over medium heat until it is thick. As the sauce thickens, it will become very stiff. Use a firm, whipping stroke to keep the sauce smooth. Simmer the sauce another 2–3 minutes while stirring vigorously. Remove from the heat and transfer the mixture to a bowl. Cover tightly and refrigerate until thoroughly chilled.

2. When the starch mixture is chilled, prepare the almond mixture. Blanch the almonds by plunging them into boiling water for 30 seconds. Drain them in a colander and

rinse with cold water. Remove the skins by squeezing the wide end of each almond. The nut should slide out easily.

3. Place the almonds in a blender along with the soymilk, maple syrup, and water, and process until smooth. Break the chilled starch mixture into chunks and add one piece at a time to the blender, continuing to whip at high speed until smooth.

4. Spoon the pudding into parfait glasses or individual serving bowls, cover tightly, and refrigerate until ready to serve.

CALLS FOR:
Gluten

SUGGESTED
COOKING METHOD:
Deep-frying

YIELD:
About 30 puffs
(1 inch in diameter)

CINNAMON-CHESTNUT PUFFS

These deep-fried doughnut-like puffs are rolled in cinnamon-seasoned chestnut flour, crushed walnuts, and a natural sweetener. It's a great way to use up a small amount of gluten.

½ cup gluten
Oil for deep-frying
3 tablespoons chestnut flour
2 tablespoons crushed roasted walnuts
1 tablespoon maple granules (maple sugar),
or other natural, unrefined granulated sugar
½ teaspoon cinnamon

1. Heat 2–3 inches of oil in a 3- or 4-quart saucepan. Pinch off ½-inch pieces of gluten and drop them gently, one by one, into the hot oil. Deep-fry the puffs until they are golden and crispy (2–3 minutes or less). Transfer to paper towels.

2. While the puffs are cooking, combine the chestnut flour, nuts, maple granules, and cinnamon in a small bowl.

3. While the cooked puffs are still hot, roll them in the flour mixture. Set the coated puffs on a plate to cool before serving.

MAPLE FUDGE PUDDING

CALLS FOR:
Thick starch

YIELD:
About 4 cups

You'll enjoy this delicious dessert, especially if you're a lover of old-fashioned chocolate pudding. You can experiment with this basic preparation to create other flavors, as well. It can also be used as a thick sauce for topping ice cream, cake, and such desserts as Almond Essence Whip (page 163).

1 cup water
3 ounces (3 squares) unsweetened baker's chocolate
1½ cups vanilla soymilk or vanilla Rice Dream beverage
½ cup maple syrup
¼ cup rice syrup
½ cup thick starch (from making homemade gluten)
1 teaspoon vanilla extract

1. In a medium saucepan, heat the water and chocolate together over a medium flame. Stir occasionally until the chocolate has melted. Set aside to cool.
2. Combine the soymilk, maple syrup, and rice syrup, and add it to the chocolate mixture. Heat over medium-low heat, stirring constantly, until the sauce is almost boiling. Reduce the heat to low, add the thick starch, and continue to stir until the sauce has thickened. Add the vanilla and simmer for 10 minutes, stirring constantly.
3. Pour the pudding into individual serving bowls (or one large bowl) and serve either hot or cold. Covered and refrigerated, the pudding will last up to four days.

COCONUT-LEMON COOKIES

CALLS FOR:
Thick starch

YIELD:
30–33 cookies
(3–4 inches in diameter)

Crispy on the edges and chewy in the center, these large, flavorful cookies are easy to assemble and take only ten minutes to bake.

2 cups whole wheat pastry flour
1 teaspoon baking powder
½ teaspoon sea salt
1½ cups shredded unsweetened coconut
Finely minced zest from 3 lemons (about 2 teaspoons)
¼ cup plus 1 tablespoon corn oil
1 cup thick starch (from making homemade gluten)
½ cup plus 2 tablespoons maple syrup
½ cup barley malt syrup
1½ teaspoons lemon extract
¼ teaspoon vanilla extract

About Sweeteners

Unrefined sweeteners such as maple syrup and barley and rice malt syrups are more nutritious than white sugar and refined brown sugar. Unrefined sweeteners contain trace amounts of minerals and other nutrients, making them ideal to use in wholesome desserts.

1. Preheat the oven to 300°F. Lightly oil two cookie sheets and set aside.
2. In a large bowl, sift together the flour, baking powder, and salt. With a fork, mix in the coconut and lemon zest. Add the corn oil, and mix it with the flour mixture to form pea-size balls.
3. In a separate bowl, combine the starch, maple syrup, barley malt syrup, and lemon and vanilla extracts. Mix well until smooth, then add this to the flour mixture. Using a spoon, stir well to form a smooth batter. Let the batter rest for about 10 minutes.
4. Drop tablespoons of the batter, about 2 inches apart, onto the prepared cookie sheets (about 6–8 cookies per sheet). Place in the oven and bake until the edge of each cookie is golden brown, slightly darker than the rest of the cookie (about 10 minutes).
5. Transfer the hot cookies to a rack. After they cool, the cookies will be crispy on the edges and chewy in the center.

BANANA DREAM PUDDING

A sprinkling of toasted shredded coconut on this banana pudding will transport you to a tropical isle. Quick to prepare, this dessert is delicious served warm or chilled.

CALLS FOR:
Thick starch and clear starch water

YIELD:
About 6½ cups

1 cup almonds
2½ cups clear starch water (from making homemade gluten), or 2½ cups plain water
2–3 bananas
1¾ cup vanilla soymilk or vanilla Rice Dream beverage
Pinch sea salt
1 teaspoon vanilla extract
½ cup maple syrup
1 cup thick starch (from making homemade gluten)
½ cup unsweetened shredded coconut

1. Blanch the almonds by plunging them into boiling water for 30 seconds. Drain them in a colander and rinse with cold water. Remove the skins by squeezing the wide end of each almond. The nut should slide out easily.
2. In a blender, place the blanched almonds along with the clear starch water, and blend until smooth. Transfer to a large saucepan and set aside.
3. Next, place the bananas, soymilk, and thick starch in the blender and process until smooth. Add this to the almond mixture in the saucepan. Heat slowly, and stir gently to combine the ingredients well. Add the salt, vanilla extract, and maple syrup. Simmer for 20 minutes, stirring frequently, until the mixture is thick and creamy.
4. While the banana-almond mixture is cooking, toast the coconut in a heavy frying pan that has been set over low to medium-low heat. Stir constantly and shake the pan back and forth periodically for even toasting.
5. Pour the pudding into individual serving bowls or cups and sprinkle with toasted coconut. Serve chilled or at room temperature.

DATE-NUT FILLED PUFFS

CALLS FOR:
Gluten

SUGGESTED
COOKING METHOD:
Baking

YIELD:
12 filled puffs

These unusual puffs are made from gluten that is wrapped around a date-nut filling and then baked. Glazing the puffs with a little maple-orange syrup before baking adds a sweet coating.

1 cup gluten
½ cup pecans, almonds, walnuts, peanuts, or filberts
½ cup chopped dates
2 tablespoons barley malt syrup
¼ teaspoon vanilla
Pinch sea salt
3 tablespoons orange juice

GLAZE
2 tablespoons maple syrup
1 tablespoon corn oil
1 tablespoon orange juice

1. To prepare the filling, crush the nuts with a rolling pin or grind them coarsely in a blender or food processor. Place the nuts in a medium saucepan along with the dates, barley malt syrup, vanilla, salt, and orange juice. Combine the ingredients well, and heat them over a low heat while stirring to prevent sticking. Simmer the mixture 2–3 minutes, remove from the heat, and set aside to cool.
2. Preheat the oven to 350°F. Lightly oil a large baking sheet and set aside.
3. Cut the gluten into 12 equal pieces. Working with one piece at a time, stretch the gluten until it is as large as you can make it without tearing it. Holding the stretched gluten down with one hand, place 2–3 teaspoons of filling on one-third of the piece. Fold the other side of the gluten over to enclose the filling, then press the edges together. Allow the filled pieces to rest for a minute, then arrange them about 2 inches apart on the prepared baking sheet.
4. Prepare the glaze by combining the maple syrup, corn oil, and orange juice. Brush this glaze on top of the filled gluten.
5. Bake for about 15 minutes. Remove the puffs from the oven, brush with a little more glaze, and place on a rack to cool.

New "Good-Old Chocolate Pudding" with Carob

CALLS FOR:
Thick starch and
clear starch water

YIELD:
8 cups

This version of chocolate pudding calls for carob as well as chocolate.

6 cups clear starch water (from making gluten),
or 6 cups plain water
2½ cups thick starch (from making gluten)
¾ cup maple syrup
1½ cups vanilla soymilk or vanilla Rice Dream beverage
7 tablespoons carob powder
1½ squares unsweetened baker's chocolate,
grated or shaved
¼ teaspoon sea salt
2 teaspoons vanilla extract

1. In a large saucepan, combine the clear starch water with the thick starch and blend until smooth. Stir in the maple syrup and half the soymilk. Set aside.
2. In a small mixing bowl, make a smooth paste by combining the rest of the soymilk with the carob powder (add the liquid little by little while mixing constantly). To this mixture, add the chocolate.
3. Add the carob-chocolate mixture to the starch mixture in the saucepan. Over medium heat,* stir continuously to mix well as the sauce thickens. Add the salt and vanilla, and continue to stir until the mixture is smooth, shiny, and runs off the spoon in a thick sheet.
4. Reduce the heat and simmer, partially covered, for 15–20 minutes. Pour the pudding into individual cups and chill before serving.

* Heat that is too high will cause starchy lumps. Be patient.

MANUFACTURERS OF SEITAN AND SEITAN PRODUCTS

Within the past few years, seitan has become an increasingly popular item with natural foods advocates. More and more companies are making seitan and prepared foods with seitan as a major ingredient. In one form or another, this vegetarian meat-like product is available in natural foods stores throughout the United States, Canada, and Europe.

Although the seitan industry is still in its infancy, there are a growing number of companies involved in the manufacturing of seitan and seitan products. Improved technology, reduced retail pricing, and ingenious cooks are all responsible for helping seitan become the "tofu of the 90s."

Some of the largest seitan manufacturers, whose products you are likely to see in natural foods stores, are presented below.

Upcountry Seitan. Founded in 1981 by Win Donavan, Upcountry Seitan is one of the oldest seitan-manufacturing companies in the United States. The company, owned and managed by Sandy Chianfoni since 1983, is located in Lenoxdale, Massachusetts. The high-quality seitan produced at Upcountry is made from 100 percent organic whole wheat flour and comes in three tamari-flavored varieties—regular, organic, and low-salt. Large chunks of Upcountry's seitan are packaged in tubs, like some tofu, and sold fresh in natural foods stores (and some supermarkets) in the New England area. This seitan is also available frozen in natural foods stores throughout the United States.

Ivy Foods. When Mark and Mira Blue Machlis, along with a few friends, opened the Sun Bun Cafe in Salt Lake City, Utah, their vegetarian Sun Burger was born. The popularity of this item encouraged the Machlis' to develop their seitan business and product line. In April of 1991, the first large-scale exposure of their products took place at the Natural Foods Expo in Anaheim, California. The positive response prompted the birth of Ivy Foods and MeatofWheat frozen seitan products.

Five styles of MeatofWheat are currently available in most natural foods stores—Hearty Original (large chunks of seitan that are suitable for slicing or cutting into cubes), Sun Burgers (the original burger), Grilled Burgers (smokey-flavored), Chicken-Style (large shredded pieces that resemble boneless chicken cutlets), and Sausage-Style (spicy-flavored ground seitan). Unlike some other non-meat burgers, Sun Burgers and Grilled Burgers are 100 percent vegan.

Sold also through mail order, MeatofWheat is available in one-pound packages (ten-pound minimum), as well as five-pound "sampler" packs. This product is shipped frozen. Once thawed, it will stay fresh in the refrigerator for seven to ten days. (See page 175 for mail-order address.)

Arrowhead Mills. For over thirty years, Arrowhead Mills has been a major supplier of high-quality natural foods. Founders Frank and Marjorie Ford are true pioneers of the natural foods movement and have been instrumental in its growth. In addition to its whole wheat flours, Arrowhead Mills now offers two new products for making homemade seitan—Vital Wheat Gluten and Seitan Quick Mix.

Vital Wheat Gluten is extracted from whole wheat through a water-washing procedure without the use or addition of chemicals. This product is a useful ingredient when a very dense, firm seitan is desired.

Seitan Quick Mix is a convenient alternative to making seitan from your own combination of flours. Made of Vital Wheat Gluten, organic stone-ground wheat flour, and teff flour, Seitan Quick Mix combines the perfect blend of ingredients for making gluten. Although preparing seitan from this mix may be less involved than the traditional method, the actual cooking time is the same.

The Bridge. Under the management of Steve LaPenta, The Bridge, in Middletown, Connecticut, has been producing seitan commercially since 1980. Made of 100 percent organic whole wheat flour, and flavored with kombu sea vegetable, soy sauce, and ginger, The Bridge's seitan is sold fresh in natural foods stores throughout New York and the New England area. Although a Hobart mixer is used for the kneading, the gluten is extracted through a hand-washing process.

Knox Mountain Farm. Wheat Balls, a boxed "instant" seitan product, is produced by Knox Mountain Farm, a small company located in New Hampshire. One 8.5-ounce box of Wheat Balls produces two pounds of the cooked product. Larger quantities are available for commercial production.

Other dry instant mixes produced and distributed by Knox Mountain Farm are Chick 'n Wheat (vital wheat gluten, chickpea flour, herbs, and spices), and Not-So Sausage (vital wheat gluten, ground fresh organic wheat berries, herbs, and spices).

White Wave Soyfoods. White Wave Soyfoods, located in Boulder, Colorado, has recently added ready-to-eat seitan to its product line. White Wave seitan is "traditionally seasoned" with ginger, garlic, onion, kombu, and soy sauce. Two four-ounce servings of the seitan come packaged with seasoned broth.

Lightlife Foods. Lightlife "Savory Seitan" comes in two flavors— teriyaki and barbecue. Both types are ready-to-eat and need no additional seasoning. Two four-ounce servings of the seitan come packaged with enough broth to use as a sauce. Lightlife Foods, producers of vegetarian foods since 1979, is located in Greenfield, Massachusetts.

MAIL-ORDER DISTRIBUTORS

The following companies are reputable mail-order distributors of natural foods. They provide high-quality ingredients for making seitan and/or the ready-made product itself. Call or write for free a catalog.

Arrowhead Mills
PO Box 2059
Hereford, TX 79045
(800) 749-0730
(806) 364-0730

**Gold Mine Natural
  Food Company**
1947 30th Street
San Diego, CA 92102-1105
(800) 475-FOOD

Ivy Foods
7613 South Prospector Drive
Salt Lake City, UT 84121
(800) 280-1313
FAX (801) 943-7311

The Mail Order Catalog
PO Box 180
Summertown, TN 38483
(800) 695-2241
(615) 964-2241

Maine Coast Sea Vegetables
RR 1, Box 78
Franklin, ME 04634
(207) 565-2907

**Mountain Ark
  Trading Company**
PO Box 3170
Fayetteville, AR 72702
(800) 643-8909
(501) 442-7191

Walnut Acres
Walnut Acres Road
Penns Creek, PA 17862
(800) 433-3998
(717) 837-0601

BIBLIOGRAPHY

Belleme, John and Jan Belleme. *Cooking with Japanese Foods: A Guide to the Traditional Natural Foods of Japan*. Garden City Park, NY: Avery Publishing Group, 1993.

Child, Julia and Simone Beck. *Mastering the Art of French Cooking*, Vol. II. New York: Alfred A. Knopf, 1983.

Colbin, Annemarie. *The Book of Whole Meals*. New York: Ballentine Books, 1983.

Estella, Mary. *Natural Foods Cookbook*. Tokyo and New York: Japan Publications, 1985.

Goldstein, Joyce. *Back to Square One*. New York: William Morrow & Company, 1992.

Grabhorn, Robert. *A Commonplace Book of Cookery*. San Francisco, CA: North Point Press, 1985.

Kushi, Aveline. *Aveline Kushi's Complete Guide to Macrobiotic Cooking for Health, Harmony, and Peace*. New York: Warner Books, 1985.

Law, Ruth. *The Southeast Asia Cookbook*. New York: Donald I. Fine, 1990.

Lin, Florence. *Florence Lin's Chinese Vegetarian Cookbook*. Boulder, CO: Shambhala Publications, 1976.

McGee, Harold. *On Food and Cooking: the Science and Lore of the Kitchen.* New York: Charles Scribner's Sons, 1984.

Miller, Gloria Bley. *The Thousand Recipe Chinese Cookbook.* New York: Antheneum Publishers, 1966.

Moulton, LeArta. *The Gluten Cookbook.* Provo, UT: The Gluten Company, 1986.

Ranhill, June. *The El Molino Cookbook.* City of Industry, CA: El Molino Mills (division of ACG Company), 1976.

Robertson, Laurel. *Laurel's Kitchen Bread Book.* New York: Random House, 1984.

Rombauer, Irma S. and Marion Rombauer Becker. *The Joy of Cooking.* Indianapolis, IN: Bobbs-Merrill Company, 1964.

Rosso, Julee and Sheila Lukins. *The Silver Palate Cookbook.* New York: Workman Publishing Company, 1979.

Shandler, Nina and Michael Rawson. *Make All the Meat You Eat from Wheat.* New York: Wade Publishers, 1980.

Shurtleff, Wiliam and Akiko Aoyagi. *The Book of Tofu.* Berkely, CA: Ten Speed Press, 1983.

Whole World Cookbook. Editors of *East West Journal.* Wayne, NJ: Avery Publishing Group, 1984.

Yoneda, Soei. *Good Food from a Japanese Temple.* Tokyo, New York, and San Francisco: Kodansha International, 1982.

INDEX